GOVERNORS STATE UNIVERSITY LIBRARY

S0-ARL-914
3 1611 00312 3343

WITHDRAWN

Mainstreaming in the Media Center

by Joyce Petrie

UNIVERSITY LIBRARY

GOVERNORS STATE UNIVERSITY

PARK FOREST SOUTH, ILL.

ORYX PRESS
1982

OCT 1 9 1982

The rare Arabian Oryx is believed to have inspired the myth of the unicorn. This desert antelope became virtually extinct in the early 1960s. At that time several groups of international conservationists arranged to have 9 animals sent to the Phoenix Zoo to be the nucleus of a captive breeding herd. Today the Oryx population is nearing 300 and herds have been returned to reserves in Israel, Jordan, and Oman.

Copyright © 1982 by The Oryx Press
2214 North Central at Encanto
Phoenix, AZ 85004

Published simultaneously in Canada

All rights reserved
No part of this publication may be reproduced or transmitted in any form or by any means, electronic or mechanical, including photocopying, recording, or by any information storage and retrieval system, without permission in writing from The Oryx Press

Printed and Bound in the United States of America

Library of Congress Cataloging in Publication Data

Petrie, Joyce.
    Mainstreaming in the media center.

    Bibliography: p.
    Includes index.
    1. Instructional materials centers—United States—Service to the handicapped.   2. Mainstreaming in education—United States.   I. Title.
    Z711.92.H3P47   027.8   82-2182
    ISBN 0-89774-006-8   AACR2

Z
711.92
, H3
P47
1982
c. 1

UNIVERSITY LIBRARY
GOVERNORS STATE UNIVERSITY
PARK FOREST SOUTH, ILL.

Contents

Preface

Historically, most school library media specialists have had only limited opportunities and no training for working with disabled students. Their contacts have been restricted to those students who were able to make their needs known or to special education classes brought into the media center for stated activities such as storytelling. Many disabled students who were segregated into special programs have not had the opportunity to make use of the media center at all.

In recent years, 2 major forces which afforded the media specialist greater opportunities and stronger capabilities for working with disabled students have influenced the educational scene. The first was legislation for the disabled. In 1975, landmark federal legislation was passed, entitled the "Education for all Handicapped Children Act," (PL 94-142), which mandated that disabled children be educated in the least restrictive environment, that is, that to the maximum extent possible they be integrated (mainstreamed) into regular classrooms and other regular public school settings. The direct implication is that educators in all fields and at all levels will want to be prepared to revise and increase their services to those children and youth who are now being mainstreamed into their programs. This has required a commitment from all educators, including media specialists, to develop new skills and knowledge in their areas of expertise as they relate to the needs of disabled students.

The second influence has been a trend in education toward *individualized, mediated* instruction. Individualized education is that which is carefully matched to the individual's developmental status and needs; it may include group as well as individual (solitary) activity, according to Maynard C. Reynolds and Jack W. Birch in *Teaching Exceptional Children*, (Reston, VA: 1977, p. 53). Mediated instruction is the process of matching as closely as possible the most appropriate print and nonprint materials and related equipment to the unique learning needs of a student in order to meet instructional goals and objectives. Individualized mediated instruction has provided greater opportunities for media specialists and teachers to accommodate the individual needs of disabled and nondisabled students through more effective use of instructional media. In order to individualize instruction, the media specialist must be involved in curriculum development and instructional design, which in turn, has given the media specialist a more integral role in the instructional program for the entire school and has given the media program stronger capabilities for accommodating diverse needs.

In response to the mandates of PL 94-142, the following needs have been identified:

1. *Disabled students* need to have access to more extensive media services as part of their educational program, the opportunity to be placed in the least restrictive environment, and the opportunity to interact with nondisabled peers as they use the school's media services and facilities.

2. *Media personnel* need to be more knowledgeable about the media-related needs of disabled students and the ways to use, adapt, and supplement media resources to meet those needs. They need to be involved in instructional design and the development of Individualized Education Programs (IEPs) for disabled students. They need tools to help them assess the strengths and weaknesses of their programs and guidelines for developing plans to make appropriate revisions in those programs.

3. *Teachers and administrators* need to be more knowledgeable regarding media methods, techniques, programs, services, materials, and equipment for use with disabled students, and they need to know about the role that the media specialist can perform in assisting them in all these areas.

4. *School districts, regional education agencies and state departments of education* need to have available to them a variety of tested operational models, strategies, and procedures for increasing the usability of media centers and for developing programs and policies in support of the media needs of disabled students.

This book has been developed in response to those needs.

Following the passage of PL 94-142 there has been a growing recognition by library media personnel that the media center and the media specialist have important roles in the education of disabled students. However, a review of the literature on media services to disabled students has revealed few materials which media personnel could use to facilitate this process.

In 1978, a project called "Media and Mainstreaming" was developed by the author under the auspices of Portland State University, School of Education, Program in Educational Media. The purposes of this project were to explore the media-related needs of mainstreamed disabled students and to develop a model, practical guidelines, and assessment tools to help media personnel develop quality media programs to meet those needs. This project was funded for 2 years, 1978–80, by the U.S. Office of Education, Library Research and Demonstration Program.

During Phase I of this funding period, the project staff worked with a task force committee of building- and district-level media specialists and special educators to develop a preliminary set of contents for a book of guidelines, a model for a media program which would meet the needs of disabled students, instruments for assessing a school's existing program, and strategies for developing a plan of action to make the program responsive to disabled students and those who work with them.

In Phase II of the project, the materials developed in Phase I were revised, field-tested, and evaluated by media specialists in Oregon and in 6 states across the country (Georgia, Indiana, Iowa, Michigan, South Dakota, and Washington). Based upon these evaluations, additional revisions were made.

Following Phase II, the materials were further revised and combined to form this book.

Acknowledgements

Thanks are due to many people who have helped in so many ways. The author is grateful for the input, evaluation, and directional advisement received from the Media and Mainstreaming Project's national advisory committee of 3 media professionals and 3 special education professionals of national prominence, and from its university advisory committee of media and special education professionals from Portland State University and the Oregon State Department of Education. In addition, thanks are extended to the readers, 18 task force committee members, the 95 media specialists who completed the field testing, and the many individuals, schools, and school districts who offered the support and services which made this project a success. Special thanks go to project staff members Linda Whitmore, Judie Foster, and Linda M. Schmoldt. I wish to particularly thank Donald P. Ely and Phyllis Hochstettler for their helpful and constructive criticism and continuing encouragement and Patrice O'Donovan, who served as research assistant and volunteer co-worker. I also thank Anne Thompson and the Oryx Press for their assistance. Finally, special thanks must go to my husband, Ronald G. Petrie, who has been patient, helpful, and enthusiastic through all stages of the book's development.

Phase I (1978–1979) Project Staff

Linda Whitmore, Assistant Director; Linda M. Schmoldt, Research Assistant; and Kathie Thornton-Jones, Graduate Assistant.

Phase II (1979–1980) Project Staff

Judie Foster, Assistant Director; Linda M. Schmoldt, Research Assistant; and Sheila Blank, Graduate Assistant.

After Phase II

Patrice A. O'Donovan, Research Assistant.

National Advisory Committee

Clifford D. Baker, University of Northern Colorado; Roland G. Billings, Ann Arbor (MI) Public Schools; Donald Ely, ERIC Clearinghouse on Information Resources/Syracuse University; Wayne Lance, Office of the Santa Clara County (CA) Superintendent of Schools; Peggy L. Pfeiffer, Lafayette (IN) School Corporation; and Mel Weishahn, University of Northern Colorado.

University Advisory Committee

Steve A. Brannan, Portland State University; Marilyn Clark, Portland State University; Allan F. Frazier, Portland State University; Diane Gutman, Portland State University; David Martinez, Portland State University; Ray S. Rothstrom, Oregon Department of Education; Cheryl Ann Scanlon, Portland State University; and Lyle Wirtanen, Oregon Department of Education.

Project Task Force

The following media specialists and special educators in Oregon contributed to the first draft of this manual. Their participation is greatly appreciated. Larry Brown, Child Services Center; Philip F. Corson, North Clackamas School District; Jorie L. Gibson, Milwaukie Elementary School; Hazel Graham, Sunset High School; Thomas Green, West Linn High School; Nancy Harden, Sunset Valley Elementary School; Vern E. Hess, Clackamas County Education Service District; Gail N. Kish, Cedar Park Intermediate School; Pamela Maben, Kinnaman School; Rebecca Macy, Oak Grove Elementary School; Toni Martinazzi, Grant High School; Jerry Nutt, Beaverton Public School District; Suzanne K. Peterson, Lauralhurst Elementary School; J. Normandie Phelps, Campbell Elementary School; Allan D. Quick, West Linn School District; Stella Satern, Oregon City School District; Larry W. Seachris, West Linn School District; and Lisa Thomas Turpel, Multnomah County.

Readers/Editors

Cynthia R. Callis, Geraldine Clark, Donald Ely, Margaret Geisler, Hazel Graham, Phyllis Hochstettler, Irene Richman, Trudy Williams, and Mary Zell.

Introduction

Mainstreaming in the Media Center has been written to be used primarily by you, the elementary, junior, or senior high school library media specialist, as a set of guidelines for assessing current media center programs and for developing and implementing modifications to those programs so that they will be in compliance with PL 94-142, the Education for All Handicapped Children Act. While written especially for the school media specialist, it is highly recommended that the book be read and used by other school personnel or interested persons— whether you are an administrator, classroom teacher, special educator, aide, or parent—in order to understand the special role and responsibilities of the school library media specialist in helping to make mainstreaming a success in the media center and in the school.

PART I

Part I of this book briefly describes basic background information about the relationship of fundamental human rights to the federal legislation which has mandated equal educational opportunities in the least restrictive environment for disabled children and youth. Implementing this legislation in school districts throughout the nation has resulted in what is now popularly known as mainstreaming.

PART II

The belief that the school library media center is the learning center of the school is strongly emphasized throughout this book. As the center of the school, it is the natural, logical place for mainstreaming to occur. In Part II, a review of all areas of a comprehensive media center program describes practical ways that this philosophy can be applied to meeting the special media-related needs of disabled students and those who work with them.

PART III

The 7 chapters in Part III are devoted to brief descriptions of each type of disabling condition as listed in PL 94-142. Each chapter contains specific ways the media specialist can use existing, altered, and/or new materials and equipment in the media center collection to accommodate the special needs of disabled students.

At the end of each chapter, a listing of resources is provided to assist in gathering information for the school's general and professional collections. Relevant organizations are also listed with addresses so that you can write for fact sheets, brochures, and other publications and inquire about additional services provided.

PART IV

An assessment instrument and related materials are provided in Part IV for use in assessing your media center program in terms of how effectively it is currently meeting the needs of mainstreamed disabled students. After completing the assessment, you can then refer to Parts I, II, and III for practical strategies and suggestions, both general and specific, for developing and implementing a plan of action for modifying your existing program according to the particular types of disabled students in your school. Use this book as a guide; take and apply only what is relevant to your own situation.

TERMINOLOGY

Some basic terminology used throughout this book is defined below.

Disabled/Handicapped. There is considerable controversy concerning the use of such words as disabled, handicapped, impaired, deficient, exceptional, or special. In this book, a "handicap" is defined as a situation created by the physical and psychological barriers which limit the functioning of a person with a "disability." Given this definition, a person can have a "disability" and a "handicap" interchangeably because (1) "handicapped" is the term used in PL 94-142; (2) both disability and handicap seem to have frequent and interchangable usage in the literature and in special education circles; and (3) it is assumed that the need for this book arises from the fact that for many students their disabilities have resulted in their being handicapped by a lack of programs to meet their educational needs.

PL 94-142 defines handicapped children as "being mentally retarded, hard of hearing, deaf, speech impaired, visually handicapped, seriously emotionally disturbed, orthopedically impaired, other health impaired, deaf-blind, multihandicapped or having specific learning disabilities, who because of those impairments need special education and related services."[1] Chapters 10–16 of this book are addressed to those specific conditions. Deaf and hard-of-hearing students are treated in a single category, and orthopedically impaired and other health-impaired students in another, since in relation to the media center the concerns are similar. Suggestions for working with multihandicapped students should come from the student's special education teacher. The category of deaf-blind is not addressed here because there is a low incidence of deaf-blind students being mainstreamed; in such a case, the special education or resource teacher should be consulted. In Chapters 10–16, PL 94-142's definition of each specific disability covered in the chapter is given; however, the definition in no way *completely* describes any particular student.

Mainstreaming. This is a popular term referring to the practice of educating disabled students along with students without disabilities. In interpreting PL 94-142's mandate for the "least restrictive environment," this means that to the maximum extent possible, disabled students are included in regular classrooms and other regular public school settings. For some students, special classes, services, and teachers will constitute their least restrictive environment. Such students, for the purposes of this book, will also be considered mainstreamed and users of the media center.

Media. This term refers to all print and nonprint materials and accompanying technology used in the educational program of the school. Media include such materials as books, periodicals, pamphlets, pictures, instructional games, slides, filmstrips, audiotapes and records, kits, films, transparencies, videotapes and discs, and microcomputer programs; plus equipment such as projectors, audio and videotape recorders and players, microcomputers, cameras, magnetic card readers, calculators, production equipment; and specialized equipment or equipment adapters for use by students with special needs.

Media Center. Depending upon the school district, the media center may be called a school library media center, an instructional materials center, a learning materials center, a library, an educational media center, or any title that designates an area where print and nonprint materials for general school usage are housed and administered. Satellite areas such as math or science resource rooms may be included as part of the media center. Special education resource rooms, where special curricular items are housed and where tutoring and remedial teaching are scheduled throughout the day, are usually considered outside the scope of the media center.

Media Specialist. Titles such as librarian, instructional materials specialist, learning resource specialist, library media specialist, and educational media specialist are synonymous and reflect the changing role of the individual who has broad professional preparation in print and nonprint forms of communication and the accompanying technology. Media specialists are professionally trained teachers with additional professional training in library media.

Mediation. Mediation is the process of identifying, creating, and using the most effective media resources to implement the teaching and learning process, taking into consideration the individual learning styles and needs of the students.

REFERENCE

1. U.S. Department of Health, Education, and Welfare, Office of Education, "Education of Handicapped Children, Implementation of Part B of the Education of the Handicapped Act," *Federal Register* 42, no. 163, 23 August 1977, p. 42478.

PART I
Background and Context

Chapter 1
Mainstreaming

MAJOR COMPONENTS OF PL 94-142

PL 94-142, the Education for All Handicapped Children Act, was signed into law on November 29, 1975. Through this law, the Congress of the United States reinforced the civil rights of all disabled children to receive a free public education. The law authorizes funding to help states and local education agencies comply with its regulations, and it threatens financial penalties for noncompliance.

PL 94-142 mandates the right of all disabled children to a free and appropriate public education, in the least restrictive environment, which is based on individual education programs, with procedural safeguards (due process), and parental involvement. This law applies to all disabled children (ages 3–21) who require special education and related services.

PL 94-142 spells out the federal government's commitment to the education of all disabled children, specifying a plan which will ensure the rights of these children to a "free and appropriate public education." It calls for free education, protecting the students and their parents or guardians from having to pay for any portions of their educational program, except for incidental fees for such materials as textbooks and supplies for which all students in the program must pay. The law reflects the view that the best education for all children ("most appropriate" and "least restrictive") is when, to the maximum extent possible, disabled students are included in regular classrooms and other regular settings. While many disabled students will require special classes or assistance and services in a public school setting, many others will move into traditional classroom settings with some special assistance. Either situation defines the concept now popularly called mainstreaming.

ORIGINS OF PL 94-142

PL 94-142 is based on a history of landmark court decisions, civil rights and education legislation, a research rationale, and current trends toward more positive views of disabled persons. In *Brown* v. *Board of Education* (1954), the U.S. Supreme Court ruled that "separate but equal" programs and facilities are inherently unequal. The federal court in Pennsylvania (1972), as a result of the Pennsylvania Association for Retarded Children (PARC) case, ordered (1) access to free public education for all retarded students regardless of degree of retardation or associated handicaps ("zero-reject" education); (2) the education of all children, based on programs of education and training appropriate to the needs and capacities of each student; and (3) that the most integrated and most normalized programs are favored in determining appropriateness.

Shortly afterwards, the court decision in *Mills* v. *Board of Education of the District of Columbia* (1972) extended the zero-reject provision to all disabilities. In 1973, a New Orleans court added the requirement for a written individualized plan for the education and training of each disabled child.[1]

In addition to judicial precedents, civil rights and education legislation provided impetus to the formulation and enactment of PL 94-142, which is actually a revision of Part B of the earlier Education of the Handicapped Act (EHA), passed in 1970. Other sections of the EHA are still in force. The Education Amendments of 1974 (PL 93-380) contain due process provisions and also assurance of education in the least restrictive environment. Section 504, a rule promulgated by the Department of Health, Education and Welfare to carry out the intent of the Vocational Rehabilitation Act Amendments of 1973, mandates that exclusion of the disabled from any educational program be prohibited after June 1, 1977. Section 504 concerns civil rights and does not provide funding authorization, but it does mandate financial penalties for noncompliance.

Besides the court decisions and federal legislation that laid the groundwork for PL 94-142, research evidence also supported the basic tenets of the new law and the need for such legislation. Although somewhat controversial, the following research helped to support the law.

In *The Exceptional Individual*, Charles Telford and James Sawrey (cited by David Johnson and Robert T. Johnson in *Learning Together and Alone: Cooperation, Competition, and Individualization*), provided a rationale for mainstreaming and PL 94-142.[2]

Based on their research findings they believed that:

1. Studies failed to establish the effectiveness of special education classes.

2. Medically and psychologically defined diagnostic categories proved inadequate for educational purposes.

3. Irrelevant factors (social class, race, sex, etc.) were influencing class placement.
4. Stigmatization had deleterious effects upon students.

In their research, David Johnson and Robert T. Johnson supported the above 4 statements and added 2 more.[3]

1. Equal access to school resources is needed by all students.
2. Healthy social development of handicapped students requires that they be part of the mainstream of social life for children their own age.

Other trends which have led to more accepting views of the disabled and paved the way for positive legislation for disabled persons have been:

- Famous persons openly discussing disabled relatives (the Kennedy family, the Hubert Humphrey family, and others).
- Changes in the ability of regular classes to handle a greater variety of students by an emphasis on individualization in the regular classroom.
- Parents becoming more informed and parents' organizations actively working and speaking out as advocates for disabled students.
- Prominent leaders in special education questioning special class placement.
- A more widespread, active participation on the part of disabled persons in social and political issues which concern them (i.e., the forming of organizations, publications, and other media; lobbying for legislative change; etc.).

PL 94-142 is law! It is well-founded. It is past the point of testimony, lobbying, amending. The question is not *whether* disabled students should be accommodated in the regular school setting, but *how* they will be accommodated. Many schools and school personnel are struggling with the implications of this law in terms of the educational program of the school, the curriculum, and the facilities. Perhaps if we emphasize the spirit of the law, the letter of the law will be easier to uphold.

HUMANITARIAN IMPLICATIONS OF PL 94-142

PL 94-142 recognizes 2 essential points:

1. In the past disabled children and youth have not received equal educational opportunities.

2. Disabled children and youth have a right to equal educational opportunities.

The right of disabled young people to a free and appropriate education is a human right derived from the fact that first and foremost the disabled are people who have the same basic needs as everyone else, such as the need for love and friendship; acceptance as an individual; knowledge of what is expected of oneself; achievement; growth, development, and learning (mentally, physically, emotionally); helping others and feeling needed; being creative; independence; structure, discipline, and freedom; identity; security; encouragement; communication (expressive language) and being listened to; sharing; privacy, quiet, and solitude; and self-esteem.[4] These needs are not based on a person's ability to function physically. The question must be raised, "Does 'less able' mean 'less worthy'?"[5]

The belief that disabled students may need special attention causes many to urge continuation of special segregated classes, because in that setting the student can receive special consideration. Disabled people have often been given an either/or choice. If you want to be treated like everyone else, then don't expect special consideration. Or, if you want special consideration, then don't expect to be treated like everyone else.

However, it is recognized that there are many times when all people want to be treated as individuals, and to have their unique talents recognized, their creative potentials affirmed, and their individual needs met. Each person has his/her own style, beliefs, and concerns. Differences— whether they are among men and women, racial groups, age groups, or disabled and "able-bodied" persons—can be used to denigrate and destroy human potential. Or, they can be used to affirm individuality and uniqueness.

Most disabled students' educational needs can be fulfilled best through some degree of mainstreaming into the regular school setting and routine. Mainstreaming involves "the interaction and togetherness of children who otherwise would have learned and lived apart . . . ."[6] This interaction and togetherness can and should be a positive experience for teachers, as well as for disabled and nondisabled students. Disabled students are resources in the ways they can contribute to other students, to their teachers, and to their school and their society. They are resources for which time, energy, and money need to be invested to bring them to their full potential.

The process begins with exposure. Disabled students need to be allowed contact—they with the real world, the world with them—in order for them to grow in an understanding of the world and what it means to be a part of it. Mainstreaming starts this process by providing students with "access to and constructive interaction with non-handicapped peers . . . ."[7]

Much of this book is about accessibility. Students need physical access to schools and to schoolrooms (in this book, specifically the media center). Once in a room, students must have access to its space and contents. Their participation in all its programs and use of all its materials should be encouraged and facilitated. This book discusses physical and environmental barriers; access to materials; policies, rules, and procedures which may create artificial barriers; and the attitudes of the media specialist, the media staff, and other students which encourage or inhibit full participation in and utilization of the media center by the disabled student.

Achieving accessibility may require structural changes, but more often it involves openness, planning, and flexibility, and, in many instances, just plain common sense. Above all, access involves sensitivity to the student. Students can be pushed, shoved, and carried to the materials or the materials to the student. But to allow that student access with the greatest independence possible, and with the least loss of dignity, is perhaps the key to what this book is all about.

REFERENCES

1. Thomas K. Gilhool, "Changing Public Policies: Roots and Forces," *Minnesota Education* 2 (2) (Winter 1976): 9–10, 12.

2. David W. Johnson and Robert T. Johnson, *Learning Together and Alone: Cooperation, Competition, and Individualization* (Minneapolis, MN: University of Minnesota, 1978), p. 37.

3. Johnson and Johnson, p. 37.

4. Phyllis Coyne, "Resource Booklet on Recreation and Leisure for the Developmentally Disabled" (Developed for the Recreation and Leisure Skills Training Workshop at Portland State University, April 1978), p. 4.

5. James L. Paul, *Mainstreaming: A Practical Guide* (Syracuse, NY: Syracuse University Press, 1977), p. 50.

6. Eliza T. Dresang, "There Are No Other Children," *School Library Journal* 24 (1) (September 1977): 22.

7. Johnson and Johnson, p. 39.

SELECTED RESOURCES—MAINSTREAMING

Amicus. South Bend, IN: National Center for Law and the Handicapped Inc., Bimonthly. 211 W. Washington St., Suite 1900, South Bend, IN 46617.

The Center's bimonthly publication, designed to monitor and report developments in the law as they relate to the rights of handicapped individuals, specifically court cases and legislation.

Ballard, Joseph. *Public Law 94-142 and Section 504—Understanding What They Are and Are Not.* Reston, VA: Council for Exceptional Children, 1977.
Brief explanation, in question and answer format, of this legislation.

Ballard, Joseph; Nazzaro, Jean N.; and Weintraub, Frederick J. *PL 94-142, The Education for All Handicapped Children Act of 1975.* Reston, VA: Council for Exceptional Children, 1976.
A multimedia kit to help educators understand the many facets of PL 94-142. Provides 3 captioned filmstrips, 3 audio cassettes, copy of law, question and answer document, and printed copies of scripts.

Hagerty, Robert and Thomas Howard. *How to Make Federal Mandatory Special Education Work for You: A Handbook for Educators and Consumers.* Springfield, IL: Charles C Thomas Publishers, 1978.
A book providing easily understood and accurate information on PL 94-142. Chapters include role of federal, state, and local leadership.

Handicapped Requirements Handbook. Washington, DC: Federal Programs Advisory Service. Monthly. 2120 L St., N.W., Suite 210, Washington, DC 20037.
Subscription includes a *Basic 504 Compliance Guide,* plus 12 monthly supplements and newletters. Individual "Agency Requirement Chapters" are separately priced. Scope and detail of this publication would make it appropriate for a district level resource.

Hein, Ronald D., and Bishop, Milo E. *Bibliography on Mainstreaming.* 2 vols. Washington, DC: Alexander Graham Bell Association for the Deaf, 1978.
A 2-volume, 900-entry bibliography on mainstreaming, focusing on the hearing-impaired, the mentally retarded, and the visually impaired.

The Law and Handicapped Children in School. Bloomington, IN: Audiovisual Center, Indiana University, 1979.
A series of 14 videotapes that assess the history and applicability of PL 94-142. Introduces some of the problems and implications of the law.

Reynolds, Maynard C., ed. *Mainstreaming—Origins and Implications.* Reston, VA: Council for Exceptional Children, 1976.
Excellent for background information and implications of the law.

U.S. Department of Health, Education, and Welfare. Office for Handicapped Individuals. *Federal Assistance for Programs Serving the Handicapped.* Washington, DC: U.S. Government Printing Office, 1978. DHEW Pub. No. OHDS 78-22001; available through GPO.

A listing of government programs which provide assistance to handicapped persons.

Weintraub, Frederick J. *State Law and Education of Handicapped Children: Issues and Recommendations*. Reston, VA: Council for Exceptional Children, 1972.
    Good reference to the laws on mainstreaming.

Chapter 2
The Media Center Philosophy

The media center is an integral, active, teaching component of the school's total instructional program. It is designed to assist students to grow in their abilities to find, generate, evaluate, communicate, and apply information that helps them to function effectively as individuals and to participate in society.[1]

Because each student has a unique combination of needs, interests, and capabilities, a wide variety of resources and experiences are essential in satisfying his/her academic and leisure time needs. The media center, through all of its components described below, can help provide this necessary variety of learning opportunities; see Chapters 4–9 for in-depth treatment of each component.

Staff. The media staff includes the media professional(s) and all other personnel who help to operate the media center, such as aides, technicians, volunteers, or student helpers. Media specialists are professionally trained teachers with additional professional training in library media. They develop, administer, and implement the media program and work cooperatively with other teachers, administrators, and students to complement, extend, and enrich the school's instructional program.

Program. The media center program is the system by which the media staff makes the facility, equipment, and media collection accessible to the entire school community through media services, instruction, and enrichment activities.

Services. Media services are the activities which facilitate the functioning of the media center. These services include selection, evaluation, and processing of media and equipment; circulation of media and equipment; reference assistance; consultation; production; inservice activities and orientation; public relations; and special activities.

Instruction. Through a media curriculum, students are given instruction to develop competencies in media skills. These skills include (1) locating information—identifying it, selecting it, evaluating it, distinguishing it from other information, etc.; (2) using information—reading it, listening to it, viewing it, interpreting it, comprehending it, applying it, etc; and (3) communicating information—organizing it, producing it, creating it, designing it, presenting it, etc.

Media Collection. The collection includes all forms of print and nonprint materials at a variety of levels to meet the needs of students and school personnel. The materials permit a multimedia approach to teaching and learning. They support, implement, and enrich the school's curriculum, allow for individualization, and encourage further interests and study.

Equipment. The media center provides the equipment needed to make use of the collection, allowing students to retrieve and use information according to their own styles and paces.

Facilities. The physical facilities provide areas where students can read, listen, view, and produce materials; where they can explore ideas; and where they can work and learn individually and together. Facilities are flexible to allow for varied activities to take place simultaneously. Arrangement of funiture, equipment, materials, and storage promotes independent usage of resources.

Media centers have typically provided a variety of resources and experiences for nondisabled students. In order to assure that the social and educational needs of the disabled student are also met, equal access to the media center and all its components is imperative.

Because the media center is already geared to meeting the variable needs of individuals, it is a natural place for mainstreaming. When existing components of the center are not adequate for meeting disabled students' needs, those same components can often be modified or adapted for special conditions. Only occasionally will the needs of disabled students require extensive changes and new materials. And often those changes will benefit the entire school.

Today's school personnel must take a new and creative look at the media center to determine how they can further extend and enrich the media program for disabled students. The media center must be a "mainstream" in the education of all students.

REFERENCE

1. American Association of School Librarians, *Media Programs: District and School*. (Chicago: American Library Association, 1975), p. 4.

Chapter 3
A Model for Developing a Media Center Program

DESCRIPTION OF THE MODEL

This model presupposes the following basic conditions:

1. The media center is viewed as an essential and central part of the school's total instructional and curricular program.
2. The media center is designed and managed by professional media staff members who work to provide a quality program of media instruction and services which make the facility, collection, and equipment accessible to the entire school community.
3. The commitment of the media specialist, the school, and the school district is to support and defend the rights of all students to equal educational opportunities.

The model begins with a (1)* *media program* that is designed and implemented in accord with the diversified needs of each individual school.

For mainstreaming to be successful in any given media center, there must be a commitment of support from the school district, the school itself, and the media center staff. The (2) *district commitment to mainstreaming* includes a recognition of its obligation to provide an equal education to all students (including disabled students) in the district in compliance with federal law and state plans; its obligation to allot equal per-pupil expenditure; and its obligation to find additional funds for excess costs through school budget reviews, readjustments, and supplementary funds. The school district administration must be willing to cooperate with parents of disabled students, school administrators, teachers, and special educators, and administrators must be willing to supply support programs to the professional teaching and paraprofessional staff (e.g., to provide inservice

---

*Numbers in parentheses correspond to model diagram shown in Figure 1.

training, specialized materials and equipment, and/or physical adaptations to school buildings to make them fully accessible to all students).

The (3) *school commitment to mainstreaming* includes compliance with district and state plans for educating all disabled students, accountability for developing and implementing an Individualized Education Program (IEP) for each disabled student in the school, the monitoring of those plans, and the reporting to parents or guardians about each student's progress. The school expresses its philosophical commitment to mainstreaming through inservice programs for teachers and staff, awareness programs for students, the establishment of communication networks with parents and the community, and the recognition and support of the importance of nonprint, as well as print media in the education of disabled students. The school should also keep the district informed about new needs arising from the implementation of mainstreaming.

The (4) *media center commitment to mainstreaming* is expressed by the media specialist's and media staff's development of programs to accommodate all students. It includes a desire by media center personnel to grow professionally and personally through learning skills for working with disabled students and by developing positive attitudes toward those students.

Given a comprehensive media program and a district, school, and media center commitment to mainstreaming disabled students into that program, there should be a (5) *media needs assessment of mainstreamed disabled students*. This is an ongoing process as changes occur in the school's disabled population, in the needs of individual students and their teachers and the staff, and in the school curriculum.

All these needs must first be viewed in light of what the media program already has to offer, (6) *existing components*. Since disabled students are, first of all, children and young adults, many of their needs are the same as those of other students and can be met with the same resources (those which are available in the media center, the school and the school district).

Because of their various disabilities, however, these students may also have some unique needs. Often these needs can be met by adaptations and modifications to the existing program, (7) *altered components*. Perhaps additional training is necessary for a staff member, or a stairway needs a ramp, or an enlargement of a diagram must be made, or a reader is required to read a script for a silent film.

When existing or altered components cannot meet the needs of disabled students, (8) *new components* must be added. These can be borrowed, bought, or even developed.

Having a comprehensive media program supported by a district-, school-, and a media center-level commitment to mainstreaming, assessing the needs of disabled students and in light of those needs developing new uses for existing components, and making necessary alterations of selected other components and developing new components results in a (9) *comprehensive media program which meets the needs of all students and their teachers.*

Administering the media center and its program of instruction and services is based on (10) *continuing evaluation* and *program development* to meet the needs identified. If the media center needs of disabled students are still not being met, the existing program must be evaluated; it should be meeting the diversified needs of all the students. Having to make a lot of major changes and having to add many new components may indicate that the existing program is lacking in qualities needed by everyone.

The guidelines presented in this manual will show ways that media personnel can follow this model to use existing, altered, and new components to meet the media needs of mainstreamed disabled students.

FIGURE 1. Model for developing a media center program which meets the needs of all students, including disabled students mainstreamed into regular programs.

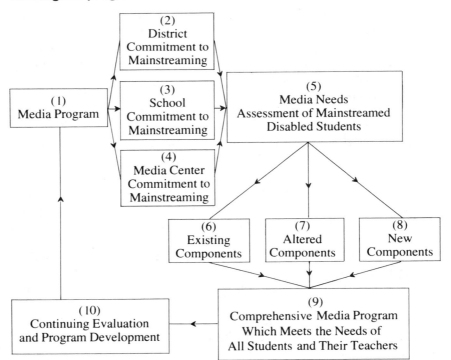

PART II
Functions of the Media Program

Chapter 4
Staff Roles

INTRODUCTION

This chapter presents steps media specialists can take to develop personal and professional competencies for filling their roles in relation to the needs of disabled students. The roles are many and varied and include managing the center and its staff; being a resource to teachers, an instructional team member, and a liaison with the administration; as well as acting as teacher and resource person for disabled and nondisabled students. Media professionals combine individual attributes, training, and experience to fill those roles and to create effective and cohesive programs.

People make mainstreaming work—not laws or court decisions, not state or district plans. Mainstreaming in the school succeeds or fails in relation to the degree of commitment of the building level staff. Successful mainstreaming within the media center depends upon the media professional.

The prospect of serving disabled students in the media center may seem to be an overwhelming responsibility. But, as D. Phillip Baker states, "Library media programs for special learners should be viewed as logical and natural extensions of our historic services and not as aberrations."[1] The media specialist who recognizes students' individual needs and interests and who strives to satisfy them does not need to make wholesale program changes to accommodate disabled students.

However, media specialists may need to become more knowledgeable and to develop positive attitudes about disabled students in order to make logical and natural extensions of their media center services to those students. Equipped with an increased understanding of disabled students, media specialists will be better prepared, and it is hoped more committed, to working with students creatively, positively, and successfully.

Becoming a media specialist who works successfully and comfortably with disabled students involves 2 attributes: acquiring professional competencies and developing or strengthening positive personal attitudes. PL

94-142 is not intended to make special educators out of all educators, media specialists included. Rather, the intention is to have educators embrace the rights of all children to equal education and to adopt some of the attitudes and strategies that make those rights a reality.

ACQUIRING PROFESSIONAL COMPETENCIES

The following suggestions will facilitate this process of information acquisition and attitude and skill development.

Become Knowledgeable about PL 94-142 and Related Legislation

A great deal of information is currently available in the professional literature concerning PL 94-142 and its ramifications. Select several of the most useful informational articles and booklets to study carefully, rather than amassing a collection too large to wade through. See the "Selected Resources" section at the end of this chapter for suggestions.

You will want to understand what mandates the laws contain, some of the reasons for such legislation, and how your school district and school plan to implement those laws. This will provide the foundation of relevance and support for implementing mainstreaming of disabled students.

Learn about the Types of Disabilities Covered under the Law

All disabling conditions are not represented in any one school; trying to study them all at one time may be counterproductive and frustrating. First, become familiar with the disabilities of the students who are in your school. Concentrate on other disabilities as time permits and as new students are admitted.

Materials that concisely list characteristics and unique needs of a particular disabling category may be of limited use. The difference in degree of impairment within any category can cover a wide range; each student is inherently different from all other students, including those identified as having the same disability. Although there may be many needs and characteristics common to students with the same disability (see Chapters 10–16), those commonalities certainly do not describe each student fully.

You will need to get to know students individually and work with the special education and classroom teachers to fully understand their needs.

Focus on the Learning Styles of Disabled Students in Your School

Understanding disabling conditions requires a basic knowledge of how those conditions may or may not influence teaching and learning. Disabling conditions can be grouped into broad categories such as intellectual, emotional, or physical impairments. The type of impairment tells little about the student's ability to learn. A student may be visually impaired and still be able to read a book with regular print, while another student with limited mobility in his/her arms may not be able to read because of an inability to hold the book. Look at the student's learning style. Disabled students have learning styles as diverse as the general population. Teaching strategies that emphasize an individual's best learning style concentrate on that student's strengths.

Discovering and learning new teaching techniques and strategies in response to the learning styles of individual disabled students consitutes another step in the media specialist's professional growth. You will usually be able to use the same scope and sequence with all students by adjusting the pace of instruction, including additional repetition and practice, and by using a variety of materials, techniques, and equipment. These will be discussed in later chapters.

SOURCES OF INFORMATION FOR DEVELOPING PROFESSIONAL COMPETENCIES

As media specialist, you can start the process of developing professional competencies for meeting the needs of disabled students by exploring the current professional literature. Much has been published in general education and media journals about mainstreaming, PL 94-142, and specific disabling conditions.

The following are suggestions for additional sources of information. See the "Selected Resources" section at the end of this chapter for addresses and annotations.

Organizations

Start by ordering a copy of the U.S. government publication, *Directory of National Information Sources on Handicapping Conditions and Related Services*. Here you will find descriptions of the purposes, activities, and services of over 270 national level organizations and federal agencies which work with and for disabled persons. The directory will be a valuable resource to you, other teachers, students, and parents.

Select several organizations from the directory which are concerned with disabilities in general (e.g., American Coalition of Citizens with Disabilities, Center on Innovation in Teaching the Handicapped, the Council for Exceptional Children, The Bureau of Education for the Handicapped). Write to them requesting information about their organizations and inquire about the services, materials, and equipment they provide. Ask for catalogs of publications and have your name placed on their mailing lists to receive newsletters and update information.

In addition, select organizations or agencies which relate to the specific disabling conditions of students in your school. For example, you might contact the American Foundation for the Blind, the National Hemophilia Foundation, or the National Epilepsy League. Find out what specific services these organizations offer, such as newsletters, educational materials, or equipment; who qualifies for their services; and what charges are made. You will discover that many free or inexpensive services are available to qualified individuals and those who work with them.

Databases

Many organizations concerned with disabilities have computer databases. While your school may not have the capabilities to do computer searches, you can arrange to have searches made through district or regional offices, or through academic or large public libraries. The following databases contain teacher- and student-use materials specific to individuals with disabling conditions.

A major source of information is the Educational Resources Information Center (ERIC) produced by the U.S. Department of Education, National Institute of Education. The ERIC database contains citations and abstracts of both the journal and the report literature in the field of education and education-related areas, with education of the disabled as one of the major subjects covered. Journal literature is abstracted and indexed in the printed *Current Index to Journals in Education* (CIJE), established in 1969. Report literature covering significant research and funded projects in education is abstracted and indexed in the printed *Resources in Education* (RIE), established in 1966. Access to the contents of both CIJE and RIE is also provided through online database vendors. If online services are not available, the media center may subscribe to the print indexes and abstracts of CIJE and RIE.

The Council for Exceptional Children's database is Exceptional Child Education Resources (ECER). ECER's extensive coverage includes all citations submitted to the Educational Resources Information Center (ERIC) system dealing with the education of disabled and gifted children, plus items that go beyond the ERIC scope, such as unpublished works and dissertations. Perhaps the media center can subscribe to the print index and abstracts that are available for accessing the materials in the ECER database system.

The National Center on Educational Media and Materials for the Handicapped (NECMMH) had been the coordinating office for a national network of regional centers. They had also developed a database called NIMIS for the specific purpose of assisting teachers, parents, and other educators to locate information about instructional materials in the field of special education. This database has since been incorporated with the National Information Center for Special Education Materials (NICSEM) and is now housed at the University of Southern California.

ACCENT is a computer-based retrieval system operated by Accent on Information, Inc. (AOI), an organization designed to help individuals with disabilities to live more effectively. Professionals working with disabled individuals would find this information useful.

Other Sources of Publications

In 1979 the National Information Center for Educational Media (NICEM) published an *Index to Non-Print Special Education Materials— Multimedia*. There are 2 volumes: One is the *Learner Volume* which abstracts materials suitable for direct instruction of disabled students; the other is a *Professional Volume* which abstracts materials for use by parents, teachers, and other educators.

Another source of information is the U.S. Department of Education, Bureau of Education for the Handicapped. In 1974 the Bureau had established a network of national special education instructional media centers which housed and circulated special education materials. Since their establishment some of these centers have been phased out, and others have been merged into regional resource centers. For an up-to-date listing of existing centers, contact the Bureau of Education for the Handicapped.

State departments of education across the country publish materials about special education and media, including informational pamphlets, monographs, and bibliographies. Ask to be placed on their mailing lists to receive materials.

The National Library Service for the Blind and Physically Handicapped (NLS), through the Library of Congress, issues 2 newsletters which often include articles about projects and new products and resources for the visually impaired and physically disabled. The newsletters, *News* and *UPDATE*, are currently free.

Other newsletters are available from universities and special education departments and associations, both locally and nationally. Many are free; others can be borrowed from association members. Special educators at schools usually belong to one or more professional associations that publish journals and newsletters.

Media specialists can also obtain information through conferences and conventions of local, state, and national special education and media organizations; through seminars and workshops sponsored by universities and colleges, school districts, state departments of education, state libraries, regional educational service districts, associations, and other agencies. Library media associations often hold conference sessions on media services for the disabled. Conferences, workshops, and seminars are usually publicized in journals, newsletters, and special mailings.

Media specialists may also consider taking college or university coursework. Introductory and survey classes in special education can provide a basic background for working with disabled students. Community colleges and continuing education programs also offer classes in special education. Many universities with library media programs now offer coursework in library services to the disabled. In the future more universities will expand their offerings to include such courses. A helpful resource for finding out what training opportunities are available in your state is the U.S. government publication *A Training and Resource Directory for Teachers Serving Handicapped Students K–12*.

Media specialist should remember that special educators in the building and district can be some of the best sources for information and assistance. In many cases, they are the fastest, most immediate resources, especially when new students arrive in the school and media center. Also, talking with students themselves will help you find out more about their interests and needs.

DEVELOPING POSITIVE ATTITUDES

Examine your beliefs, feelings, and attitudes about disabled students

In order for disabled students to function effectively and learn from media center programs, they must feel comfortable in the center and know that they are welcome there. The media specialist is responsible for conveying that welcome. No amount of professional training and knowledge of special education can make up for, or cover up, negative feelings either about disabled students themselves, or about the need for providing programs and services for them. On the other hand, positive attitudes about disabled individuals and a desire to meet their needs, coupled with a measure of common sense, will often compensate for a lack of special education expertise.

A commitment to the idea of mainstreaming is expressed verbally and nonverbally through sensitivity, flexibility, understanding, openness to communication, enthusiasm, and patience.

Disabled students, like all other students, can usually spot a phony very quickly.

> Whatever else may be impaired, handicapped children often have developed highly refined skills in evaluating the feelings of people they come in contact with. They know the difference between welcome and tolerance, between concern and obligation, between warmth and phoniness.[2]

Even the most well-meaning media specialist may be exhibiting unconscious biases and misunderstandings about the disabled by confusing sensitivity with sentimentality and pity, or by patronizing some students.

Discuss your feelings and attitudes with the special educators. They can offer suggestions, insights, and support.

Increase your knowledge about relating to disabled individuals

As in other aspects of life, changed attitudes often result from increased knowledge and understanding of a subject. Understanding the spirit and intention of PL 94-142 and learning about disabilities and their influences on teaching techniques and learning can contribute to your confidence in working with disabled students.

Many sources of information described in the section on acquiring professional competencies can likewise be agents of attitude change. College coursework, workshops, and inservices designed to provide data about disabilities, teaching techniques, etc., may also include experiential activities that heighten a nondisabled person's sensitivity to the problems faced by the disabled and provide opportunities to meet and interact with disabled individuals.

Consult with disabled students and adults about experiential activities that you could try which will give some degree of understanding of what it feels like to live with various disabilities. For instance, try using a wheelchair or crutches, not only to test the accessibility of your surroundings, but also to experience how differently other people respond to you. View a film or filmstrip without the sound; try another one unfocused. Even though many more facets of a particular disability exist than one can pretend to experience in these activities, a nondisabled person can gain at least some insight into the world of the disabled person.

A disability is only one dimension of a person's life. Besides journal articles and books intended to convey research results and technical data about disabilities, other materials are available that emphasize the person rather than the disability. One example of this type of material, taken from *Disabled USA*, describes the experiences of a blind girl, Deborah Kent, in elementary school:

> When I entered elementary school in the mid-'50's, I attended a special class for the blind in the middle of a veritable ghetto for disabled children. Almost the entire first floor of the large inner-city school was reserved for us. Besides my own class there were classes for the partially sighted, the deaf, the orthopedically handicapped, and the mentally retarded.
>
> Very early I realized I was relegated to a world meant to be separate but equal. Upstairs was where the other, normal pupils learned and played. They walked to school each day; I arrived from a neighboring town in a special taxi. During recess I was sent to play with the other handicapped children in the "kitty-coop," a tiny porch divided from the inviting hubbub of the main playground by a high wire fence. One day each Spring the school emptied as the regular students left for their annual field day—those of us in the special classes stayed behind for our annual party, given by a group of volunteers.
>
> I belonged to a Girl Scout troop in my home town, but the contact with sighted girls my own age only heightened my sense that I lived apart. Because I was only with them during our weekly meetings, I didn't share their camaraderie, which grew out of a wealth of shared adventures and private jokes. I didn't know their teachers or their boyfriends. I hadn't been in geography class when the crow flew through the window. The troop leaders worried when I went with them on camping trips—I wasn't even allowed to toast my own marshmallows. It was no fun being different. I concluded that it was better to be like everybody else.
>
> Finally, in eighth grade, I was transferred to the public school in my own neighborhood. I determined to put the world of specialness behind me, and to pass in sighted society. I directed all of my energy toward proving that I was as competent as anyone who could see. As if the peformance of difficult feats would ensure me a foothold, I learned to ride horseback, acted in school plays, and took part in a tumbling competition. They were all things I wanted to do, and I enjoyed doing them. But always I felt an extra sense of hidden triumph: I had shown them all at last.[3]

Other examples can be found in fiction, biography, and autobiography, in all formats. Criteria are given for evaluating the representation of disabled persons in print and nonprint media in Chapter 7, "The Media Collection."

Interact with disabled people

Personal experience with disabled children and adults through observations, advocacy programs, friendships, and working relationships can stimulate the development of positive feelings about the disabled. Talking to a disabled person about his/her disabilities, special needs or problems, and personal ways of coping and overcoming them contribute to one's understanding of that individual. But more important is talking as one person to another about topics other than the disability.

Since attitudinal barriers are usually more difficult to overcome than architectural barriers, the disabled usually welcome the opportunity to clarify understandings about who they are. Consult with the disabled students themselves about ways to promote understanding that are comfortable for them. One student may enjoy leading a question and answer period while another would prefer private one-to-one interaction.

One way of assessing your feelings about disabled students is to analyze specific interactions with them. It is easy to verbalize a commitment to serving all students, less so to substantiate that commitment in everyday actions. For instance, do you:

- Tease and joke with disabled students as often as you do with other students?

- Touch disabled students as much as others?

- Maintain eye contact with the disabled student?

- Sit or stand at a level or in a location that is comfortable for a disabled individual?

- Talk to disabled students about things other than media and/or their disability?

Communication between student and teacher is the most important element in the learning process. Nonverbal forms of expression contribute significantly to the process. Body language, facial expressions, eye contact, etc. all convey meaning and can either augment or contradict verbal communication. A media specialist's discomfort or displeasure with disabled students will most likely be perceived by them. This negative communication can disrupt or slow the learning process.

You may not be able to succeed in every interaction with disabled students; you may fail to communicate a direction or thought, or fail to understand a student request. Be patient with yourself! Even in unsuccessful interaction you can at least convey the message that you have tried and that you really care about succeeding. Try some of the monitoring and evaluation techniques for student-teacher interaction found on page 185 of *The Handicapped Child in the Regular Classroom*. (See ''Selected Resources'' section at the end of this chapter.)

THE MEDIA SPECIALIST AS MANAGER OF THE MEDIA CENTER

Many media specialists do not operate their media centers alone. Other professionals, paraprofessionals, paid and volunteer aides, and student helpers may be involved. All of those involved in the operation of the media center contribute to its environment, either positively or negatively.

Media center directors are responsible for seeing that the entire media center staff, both paid and volunteer, express themselves positively in relation to all students. Media specialists who work to achieve professional competencies and positive personal understandings about the disabled can serve as role models for other staff members; however, role modeling alone is not enough to ensure that those positive attitudes influence and affect others. If you are a media center director, you might consider making the same types of learning and growing activities that you have experienced available to all media center staff members.

Paid Aides

Media center aides should be encouraged to work with all students, including disabled students, and should be given opportunities to develop skills that will make their contacts with students easier and more effective. Many aides have responsibilities in the media center that involve a great deal of interaction with students. Define expectations for aides in relation to students, as well as work expectations. Ability to relate to students is an important criterion when aides are interviewed for their positions.

Media aides will need the media center director's support and instruction to work positively with disabled students. Media specialists may need to invest time and energy in helping aides develop better skills and attitudes. This will help to ensure that the media center environment remains warm and inviting for all students, even when media specialists are out of the facility.

To facilitate media center aides' personal growth and skills acquisition, media specialists can provide materials to read and information about workshops and classes that may be helpful. Aides should also be included in media center and school inservice programs dealing with mainstreaming and disability awareness.

Flexible scheduling of aide work hours or other compensation (i.e., monetary or leave time) are incentives that will encourage media aides to willingly undertake these activities. Additionally, media specialists should allow time to discuss activities, provide reinforcement, and plan with aides ways of making use of new skills and understandings.

Aides can also be assigned special roles and tasks that will meet the unique needs of some students and that take advantage of aides' talents and interests. An aide might be asked, for example, to tutor individuals who require extra help with some media skills, or to be an advocate for a group of students to meet their media needs. Media specialists should make the most of what aides have to offer, especially when aides attempt to acquire additional skills, even if doing so means adjusting traditional aide responsibilities.

Volunteers

Volunteers can assist in the media center by performing routine tasks which free the media specialist to work with more students, and by sharing special skills and talents that enrich the media program. In either case, volunteers should be assigned specific tasks or roles and should be expected to work within the policies set up for all media staff members.

Many community resource persons (who may themselves be disabled) have skills that enable them to work well and creatively with disabled students. They could be asked to assist individual students who may have unique needs not easily met in a group setting. Also, they may serve as companions for "handicapped children (who) may need someone from outside the school to communicate with—someone who is not threatening."[4]

Other volunteers may be less suited to working closely with disabled students but should, nonetheless, be expected to exhibit positive behavior and attitudes towards all students. Volunteers should be observed and evaluated to see that they are not creating a negative environment through such behaviors as insensitivity, impatience, avoidance of some students, maternalism/paternalism, and talking down to students.

Including volunteers in awareness activities planned for other media staff members and clarifying media center policies relating to disabled students will help alleviate many serious attitude problems. Volunteers who perform tasks for the media specialist at the expense of students' self-esteem and progress cannot be considered assets to the program.

Student Helpers

Students themselves can be valuable resources in the media center for performing a wide variety of tasks, while at the same time acquiring and strengthening media center and future employment skills. A well-developed student aide program involves additional work for media specialists, but carries with it rewards for both the students and media staff.

Depending on age, students can successfully take over many tasks that adult media staffers would otherwise do: equipment trafficking, film projection, production, copy services, processing, circulation activities, typing, filing, housekeeping, etc. With training students can take over tasks, freeing media professionals and paid aides to work more with students and teachers than with books, paper, or pieces of equipment. Students with adequate skills training and feelings of being needed and useful will take pride in their roles and themselves and can do very good jobs with little supervision.

As in other media services and programs, all students, including the disabled, should be considered potential student helpers. Assigning tasks to individual students should be based on their interests and aptitudes, not on an estimate of how quickly they can learn a particular task. The quality and success of a student helper program should be measured by how much learning takes place rather than the number of tasks that are performed.

As an example, one media specialist taught a retarded boy to operate an autoload 16mm film projector. The training also included moving the projector throughout the building on schedule and taking responsibility for the care of both projector and films. The returns were great: a dependable projectionist proud of his work and an equally proud media specialist who had less equipment trafficking to worry about.

But what about the student whose task is to come to the media center day after day to dust shelves? In comparison, it may seem more like marking time than learning. However, the job could entail learning such things as how to dust and what to dust, how to finish a large job systematically, where to find dust cloths and where to store dirty ones. The student may also be working on self-regulatory and employment skills: dependability, arriving on time, staying on the task, etc. What is more, this particular student may be just as proud of his/her work as the projectionist and be just as willing to continue.

Student helpers, disabled or not, should be aware of media center policies and their roles in the maintenance of a positive environment for all. Defining appropriate attitudes and behaviors is never enough. Activities and discussions aimed at developing and strengthening understanding about similarities and differences among individuals and respect for human rights and dignity should accompany skills instruction. All student helpers must contribute positively to the media center environment as a condition of their program participation; no less should be expected or tolerated.

THE MEDIA SPECIALIST AS RESOURCE TO TEACHERS

Cooperating with classroom teachers to help them identify, select, design and produce media resources for teaching and learning is a major responsibility of the media specialist. Good cooperation is not accidental; it takes time and effort.

Cooperation happens when the media specialist:

- Is available and accessible to all teachers.
- Is clearly willing to work with teachers.
- Keeps abreast of new curricula.
- Keeps records of teacher interests, plans, and needs.
- Initiates teacher contact.
- Responds to specific requests.
- Keeps teachers informed of new resources.
- Involves teachers in the selection process.

This kind of cooperation benefits all students in the school and makes both teaching and learning more relevant, interesting and rewarding. When new challenges such as mainstreaming arise, requiring new resources and new ways of adapting and utilizing the existing collection and curricula, this cooperation becomes even more essential.

Within the school, in cooperation with other teachers and special education resource persons, media specialists can initiate and organize a network to identify new and varied uses for the school's media collection.

The media specialist is often the avenue by which external resources are identified and brought into the school, either for purchase or on loan. District media and special education supervisors, as well as building-level special educators, are good resource persons to contact to help locate needed media from outside sources. Look for special education media collections in your state; some of these may be connected with teacher training institutions. Materials may be borrowed from collections at building, district, county, state, and national levels.

Professional Library

Building and maintaining a professional library collection for teachers which is comprehensive, accessible, and easily used is another aspect of the media specialist's role as a resource to teachers. The materials collected for developing professional competencies can serve as the basis for this collection. For very little investment, you can accumulate a diverse collection of interesting and practical items that will probably get more use than comprehensive texts and monographs.

Use is the measure of a good professional collection. The following suggestions will help the media specialist in promoting and expanding that usage.

1. Circulate items. Deliver specific items to teachers in response to requests or needs. But do not always wait to be asked; deliver items you think might be useful to them.
2. Distribute bibliographies on such topics as mainstreaming and disabling conditions.
3. Attach notes to periodical covers to call attention to articles relevant to mainstreaming and disabled students.
4. Develop an easy system for getting teacher suggestions on items and for sharing suggestions with other teachers.
5. Keep the professional collection up-to-date.
6. Encourage the teachers to help you and each other by filling out simple review forms on the materials they read, view, and listen to. On the basis of these reviews, you will be able to weed out useless items and direct teachers to relevant information. Ask special educators to review specific special education materials in terms of their usefulness for other teachers.

Inservice

As mainstreaming goes into effect in the school, classroom and subject area teachers may indicate they are lacking in knowledge of disabling conditions and specific techniques, materials, and equipment to use in instructing disabled students. If teachers are to be given increasing responsibility for planning educational programs for disabled students, they must be given ample support in learning how to design and carry out appropriate instructional plans. Inservice programs can be a valuable source of knowledge and support for teachers and staff working with these students.

Effective inservice programing will require the cooperation of all the specialists in the school. The media specialist can make a valuable contribution by arranging for films, tapes, other materials, and the equipment needed for the session. The media center may be the best place to hold such a program. The media specialist can reinforce the topics of the inservice session by pointing out materials in the media collection and the professional library which provide more details, background, or specific suggestions. As media specialist, you can also order specific materials, such as free pamphlets from organizations, and you can cooperate in the preparation of materials for the session.

Sometimes media specialists will develop inservice programs based specifically on instructional media: how to adapt and/or design materials for disabled students; how to produce those materials; presentations of new materials or equipment for use with disabled students; etc. Although you may not always conduct the inservice session (perhaps a guest speaker or the salesperson who sold you a product would do the presentation), you could certainly act as the instigator of the event and function as a facilitator.

The media specialist should also take part in the design of short- and long-range staff development plans on which inservice programs are based. You can help determine the need for inservice programing about mainstreaming through personal observations, by the statistics you keep on the use of the media center, or in response to direct criticism or requests for assistance; for example, consider whether disabled students use the media center. Do teachers encourage and plan to bring disabled students to the center? Do teachers request and use specialized materials and equipment? Do they know how to use them?

Inservices on mainstreaming should include activities directed at heightening awareness and sensitivity to the needs of disabled students. When possible, invite classified staff (janitors, cooks, aides, etc.) to participate in this type of inservice training. Their attitudes strongly affect the success of mainstreaming in a school.

It will probably be necessary to draw upon the expertise of a variety of resources, including disabled citizens and individuals who work with the disabled in your community. Try to achieve a balance of building-level and outside resources, as both have much to contribute.

THE MEDIA SPECIALIST AS TEAM MEMBER

Besides being a resource person to teachers, media specialists further cooperate with school faculty in designing and implementing instruction for both the classroom and media center. Extensive coordination between the two enhances learning by providing complementary instruction and varying experiences aimed at achieving specific educational goals.

Because the media center provides a more relaxed and informal setting than the classroom, the media specialist can observe and informally assess students' abilities and skill levels in nonacademic, as well as academic, areas. Based on their interaction with individual students, media specialists can give input to other teachers.

By considering themselves a part of the instructional team, media specialists can more easily keep abreast with what classroom teachers are doing, as well as learn more about individual students. In working closely with classroom and special education teachers, media specialists can obtain information about students' learning styles, their strengths and weaknesses, their habits, and their needs. Additionally, team members can provide suggestions for dealing specifically with certain students, including methods, techniques, and strategies that they have found most effective.

A new responsibility for the media specialist is contributing to the team that develops Individualized Education Programs (IEPs) for disabled students. As a media specialist, you have the training, knowledge, and expertise to work on instructional design and make suggestions for mediating that instruction for individual students. In this capacity, you can point out specific materials, relate how they have been used in various instructional situations, give ideas for new and innovative ways to use those materials, suggest appropriate commercial materials which could be purchased, and borrowing and funding sources for supplementing the collection. In addition, you can suggest alternative media formats and appropriate audiovisual equipment. When materials are not available to meet the specific goals of an IEP, you can assist in the design and production of items that will meet that need.

If you are a part of the team which plans the IEP, you will be able to integrate those goals and objectives into the media program. A copy of the IEP itself and the team members who developed it will be ready resources as you work with the disabled student.

The team approach which involves classroom teachers, special educators, and media specialists benefits all participants and most importantly, the student. Cooperative team planning results in positive, creative, and constructive ways of meeting the needs of individual students.

THE MEDIA SPECIALIST AND THE ADMINISTRATION

The school administrator—the principal—is the key to establishing the atmosphere which is necessary for mainstreaming to succeed in the school. The principal must be aware of the physical, social, emotional, and intellectual needs of disabled students, as well as the needs and concerns of the staff members who work directly with them. Perhaps the most difficult challenge for the principal is to find ways to provide additional information and inservice training for staff members and extra time for them to work with the students.

The media specialist can assist the principal by supplying information and helping to plan and carry out inservice programs for teachers. Administrators should be included with other teachers in the network for circulating professional materials and obtaining comments, evaluations, and suggestions for use. Administrators often receive materials and announcements of new materials that do not come through the media center. Take the initiative with administrators in seeing that relevant materials reach the rest of the faculty.

THE MEDIA SPECIALIST AND NONDISABLED STUDENTS

Research studies have shown that even very young children are aware of physical differences among people and that they often react negatively to physically disabled persons.[5] As they get older, children begin to distinguish, and negatively judge, intellectual and social/behavioral differences as well. Most children grow up isolated from disabled persons and have neither personal knowledge of disabilities nor one-to-one experiences with disabled individuals.

Because of mainstreaming, more students are brought into contact with disabled persons at an earlier age but not, however, early enough to prevent the development of prejudicial feelings and fears. Part of the success of mainstreaming rests in the elimination of nondisabled students' negative feelings toward their disabled peers.

Media specialists can help by providing information about handicaps and suggesting print and nonprint materials that positively represent disabled persons. (See Chapter 7, "The Media Collection.") Such materials can be utilized in ways that accustom students to seeing, hearing, and reading about the disabled in any given situation. The expectation is that students will eventually lose their fears and become more open to personal relationships with persons different from themselves.

As media specialist, you can also provide awareness activities in the media center designed to sensitize nondisabled students to the problems and feelings of their disabled peers and to help break down attitudinal barriers between them. Attitudinal changes can be addressed through literature, films, speakers, and experiential activities. (See "Selected Resources" listed at the end of Chapter 7, "The Media Collection.")

Of great importance is your attitude and behavior as a role model for students. Expressing yourself positively towards disabled students will help other students do so as well. Remember, however, that positive behavior towards the disabled means treating them like any other student. Nondisabled students will resent the disabled student who "gets away with murder."

Specialized equipment or materials designed for use by one or only a few students may be another possible source of resentment. Give special students priority use but, if possible, allow other students access as well. For very specialized equipment, such as an optical to tactile converter, invite the user to demonstrate and explain its use. At all costs, avoid labeling and limiting any item in the media center.

Media specialists should try to be open and honest with students and encourage questions and discussions about disabilities, human differences and similarities, feelings, and fears. Your attitude and approachability can help all students feel comfortable in coming to you with questions and requests for information and assistance.

THE MEDIA SPECIALIST AND DISABLED STUDENTS

Disabled students should be included in all media center activities; they should neither be left out nor isolated and labeled by separate activities. Programs should be designed so that each student can do well while being involved with other students. This can be accomplished by dividing the various aspects of an activity among the group members, making sure that each student, while being challenged, also has an opportunity for success. (See ''Group Structures'' section in Chapter 6, ''Programs—Instruction.'')

Be sure to invite disabled students to take part in awareness activities designed to promote understanding among students. In most cases, disabled students are no more tolerant of human differences than are other students. It is a myth that disabled persons are in some kind of symbiotic communion with all other disabled persons. Tell students if you will be discussing disabilities similar to theirs; ask them if they wish to participate, thereby giving them the option to accept or refuse. You may wish to check with parents about conducting such activities.

The media specialist should act as a sensitive facilitator in promoting thoughtful interaction during awareness activities or should make arrangements for professional or training facilitators to be available. Try to assure that guilt, defensiveness, and further polarization are not the outcomes of such activities.

Disabled students can also be resources for developing awareness activities for other students. They are often in tune with how people respond to them and they know how they want to be responded to. Many can articulate the changes they would like to see. Media specialists can find out how these students feel and help translate these feelings into activities for other students.

One of the central goals of PL 94-142 is to achieve a normalization of disabled students' lives; but they must also learn to cope with the many restrictions society places on all people. While efforts should be made in the media center to accommodate the disabled student, this should not be done by eliminating all rules, watering down policies, or exempting disabled students from compliance. What is important is that the students learn how to behave appropriately in varying situations, to be responsible for their actions, and to care for the property and the physical safety of themselves and others. Learning to follow rules and to work within structures, whether it is within society in general or within the media center, are essential skills for everyone.

For example, a rule for maintaining an appropriate noise level in the media center fosters consideration for others. However, what about the deaf student who may occasionally speak too loudly? While such behavior certainly should not be punishable, that student also must be made aware of the rule and why it exists, and should receive help in monitoring his/her voice level. Consistency is important. The media specialist, as a member of the team, will learn the cues other teachers use to help the student with this process.

Part of acquainting students with media center rules and standard procedures occurs through the orientation program. (See "Orientation" section in Chapter 5, "Programs—Services.") Time spent in orienting students to the media center will help disabled students to understand what is expected of them. As rules and standard procedures are developed for students to follow, keep in mind the following:

- Establish positive and reasonable expectations for students.
- Be flexible—look at alternatives and select those which best serve immediate needs.
- Be open to one-to-one interaction.

Through flexibility, openness, and equal treatment, media specialists express their beliefs that disabled students are equal members of the school community.

REFERENCES

1. D. Philip Baker and Dave Bender, *Library Media Programs and the Special Learner* (New York: The Shoestring Press, 1981), p. 175.

2. Barbara Baskin and Karen H. Harris, eds., *The Special Child in the Library* (Chicago, IL: American Library Association), 1976, p. 7.

3. Deborah Kent, "There and Back Again," *Disabled USA,* 1 (7) (1978) 14–15.

4. Ruark, Ardis and Melby, Carole. *Kangaroo Kapers or How to Jump into Library Services for the Handicapped.* (Pierre, SD: Division of Elementary and Secondary Education, 1978), p. 24.

5. Dianne Monson and Cynthia Shurtleff, "Altering Attitudes Toward the Physically Handicapped Through Print and Non-Print Media," *Language Arts* 56 (2) (February 1979), p. 165.

SELECTED RESOURCES—STAFFING

Books and Booklets to Consult

American Library Association. *Programming for Children with Special Needs*. Chicago, IL: American Library Association, 1980.

American Library Association. Association for Library Service to Children. Library Service to Children with Special Needs Committee. *Selecting Materials for Children with Special Needs*. Chicago, IL: American Library Association, 1980.

Baker D. Philip, and Bender, Dave. *Library Media Programs and the Special Learner*. New York: The Shoestring Press, 1981.
Contains case studies of exemplary media programs serving handicapped students.

Baskin, Barbara, and Harris, Karen H., eds. *The Special Child in the Library*. Chicago, IL: American Library Association, 1976.
Provides a compilation of articles relating to library media services for disabled students. Although somewhat dated, this book was a forerunner of concern about disabled children in the library. Both Baskin and Harris have continued their work in this area (see other references in Bibliography) and are names to keep in mind for quality information.

Gearheart, William R., and Weishahn, Mel. *The Handicapped Child in the Regular Classroom*. St. Louis, MO: Mosby, 1976.
Gives good basic coverage; very readable.

Heinich, Robert, ed. *Educating All Handicapped Children*. Englewood Cliffs, NJ: Educational Technology Publications, 1979.
Offers guidelines to educators for managing the changes necessitated by mainstreaming. Deals with systemwide effects of such areas as the structure of the school, the organization of teacher education, design of instruction, etc. Valuable to the media specialist as an instructional team member.

Lake, Sara, compiler. *Mainstreaming: A Special Interest Resource Guide in Education*. Phoenix, AZ: Oryx Press, 1980.
Provides an annotated bibliography surveying materials published from 1977 through February, 1980 dealing with the mainstreaming concept and its 2 related federal laws, PL 94-142 and Section 504.

Schrag, Judy A. *Individualized Educational Programming (IEP)*. Mainstreaming Series, Boston: Teaching Resources (formerly published at Austin, TX: Learning Concepts, 1977).
Facilitates an understanding of the concept of Individualized Educational Programing and describes a process for its implementation. One of 15 books available in the "Mainstreaming Series."

Thomas, Carol H., and Thomas, James L. *Meeting the Needs of the Handicapped: A Resource for Teachers and Librarians.* Phoenix, AZ: Oryx Press, 1980.

Provides a selection of essays and articles with suggestions for programs or activities appropriate for disabled students, taken from educational journals published between 1973 and 1979.

Turnbull, Ann P.; Strickland, Bonnie; and Brantley, John C. *Developing and Implementing Individualized Education Programs.* Columbus, OH: Charles E. Merrill Publishing Co., 1978.

Gives information on how to implement PL 94-142—discusses steps and mechanics for writing IEPs.

U.S. Department of Health, Education, and Welfare. Office for Handicapped Individuals. *Directory of National Information Sources on Handicapping Conditions and Related Services.* 2d ed. Washington, DC: U.S. Government Printing Office, 1980. DHEW publication no. OHDS 80-22007.

Describes the purposes, activities and services of over 270 national-level organizations and federal agencies in a comprehensive volume. Available from: Clearinghouse on the Handicapped, 400 Maryland Ave., S.W., Rm. 3106, Switzer Building, Washington, DC 20202.

Periodicals to Consult

Audiovisual Instruction. "The Role of Media in Special Education." 14 (November 1969).

Audiovisual Instruction. "Technology and the Exceptional." 21 (December 1976).

Exceptional Children. Reston, VA: Council for Exceptional Children. 8 issues per year. 1920 Association Dr., Reston, VA 22091.

Illinois Libraries. "Media/Information/Services for Exceptional Students." 59 (September 1977).

Interracial Books for Children Bulletin. "Handicappism in Children's Books." (Double Issue.) 8 (6, 7) (1977).

School Media Quarterly. "Special Education: A Continuum of Services." 6 (Summer 1978).

Teaching Exceptional Children. Reston, VA: Council for Exceptional Children. Quarterly. 1920 Association Dr., Reston, VA 22091.

Materials Useful for Inservice Programs

Baker, Clifford D., and Fowler, Barbara J. *Preparing General Educators to Work with Handicapped Students*. Greeley, CO: University of Northern Colorado, 1979.

> Provides a wide variety of field-tested teacher-training activities, step-by-step teaching suggestions, supplementary instructional materials, and an updated listing of resources for developing mainstreaming competencies for general educators. Useful resource for planning inservices.

Project STRETCH. (1980). Hubbard, 1946 Raymond Dr., Northbrook, IL 60062. (Video films.)

> Contains a series of 20 color 30-minute 16mm film or videotape programs, each with a teacher's manual. Designed as a complete inservice program, it includes concepts, strategies and subject matter materials for teaching handicapped children in regular classroom settings. Can be used with all children in varied educational settings. Manuals can be ordered separately covering such topics as assessment, peer tutoring, and learning styles.

Teacher Training in Mainstreaming. New York: EPIE (Educational Products Information Exchange) Institute, 1978. EPIE Report No. 86m.

> Gives extensive analysis on the instructional aspects of materials designed for inservice training relevant to mainstreaming. Covers 15 series of training materials. Excellent for evaluation of existing series or for designing your own training materials.

U.S. Department of Health, Education, and Welfare. *A Training and Resource Directory for Teachers Serving Handicapped Students, K-12*. Washington, DC: U.S. Government Printing Office, 1979.

> Provides a directory of national and state resources listed by state. For information, write Director of Technical Assistance Unit, Office of Program Review and Assistance, Office for Civil Rights, 330 Independence Ave., SW, Washington, D.C. 20201.

Organizations

Accent on Information, Inc. (AOI), Gillum Rd. and High Dr., P.O. Box 700, Bloomington, IL 61701.

> Provides materials and services to help disabled individuals live full and satisfying lives. Accent on Information is AOI's data retrieval system.

Bureau of Education for the Handicapped, U.S. Office of Education, Washington, DC 20202.

> Has catalogs of publications, programs, etc., including catalog of captioned films.

Council for Exceptional Children (CEC), 1920 Association Dr., Reston, VA 22091.

Send for free catalog of publications and nonprint media. Through CEC's database, ECER, the following services are offered: custom computer searches, computer search reprints, annual topic bibliographies, and quarterly indexes. CEC also publishes the periodicals *Exceptional Children* and *Teaching Exceptional Children* (see "Periodicals to Consult" above).

Educational Resources Information Center (ERIC), National Institute of Education, 1200 19th St., N.W., Washington, DC 20208.

ERIC is a nationwide information system providing access to education literature, including education of disabled students and library/media center concerns. Access to ERIC is found through (1) the *Current Index to Journals in Education* (CIJE) (Phoenix, AZ: Oryx Press, monthly with semiannual cumulations) for journal literature; (2) *Resources in Education* (RIE) (published monthly and available through the Government Printing Office, with annual cumulations published by Oryx Press) for report literature; and (3) through online database suppliers.

National Center of Educational Media and Materials for the Handicapped (NCEMMH), 356 Arps Hall, 1945 N. High St., Ohio State University, Columbus, OH 432 10.

Send for free newsletter and periodical *The Directive Teacher;* also ask for information on their resources and services.

National Information Center for Special Education Materials (NICSEM), University of Southern California, University Park, Los Angeles, CA 90007.

Send for information on their database—NICSEM/NIMIS—and order their newsletter, *Frankly Speaking,* which is currently free. See also their *NICEM Index to Non-Print Special Education Materials—Multimedia, Volume 2: Professional Volume* (1979), which abstracts materials for parents, teachers, and other educators.

National Library Service for the Blind and Physically Handicapped, Library of Congress, 129 I Taylor St., N.W., Washington, DC 20542.

Offers free services to qualified individuals. Send for information on bibliographies of their publications and specifics on services and their newsletters, *Update* and *News,* which are currently free.

National Support Systems Project, 350 Elliott Hall, University of Minnesota, Minneapolis, MN 55455.

Send for information on their publications, including their periodically revised bibliographies of books, articles and resources: Peterson, R.L. and Bass, K. *Mainstreaming: A Working Bibliography* (1977); Peterson, R. L. *Mainstreaming Training Systems, Materials and Resources: A Working Bibliography* (1977).

Chapter 5
Programs—Services

INTRODUCTION

Chapter 5 (''Programs—Services'') and Chapter 6 (Programs—Instruction'') describe ways to make the media program more responsive to the needs and interests of disabled students in the school. The media program is the system by which the media staff makes the facility, equipment, and media collection accessible to the entire school community through media services and instruction.

The chapter on services includes technical services (cataloging and processing, reference, circulation, consultation, production, public relations, orientation, and special activities (student workshops, contests, etc.). It delineates specific media services and demonstrates how minor changes can often make those services accessible to the disabled student. It also includes some of the special services the media staff can provide to help make mainstreaming a successful and positive experience. (For the service of media selection see Chapter 7, ''The Media Collection.'' Maintenance of material and equipment is covered in Chapter 8, ''Equipment.'')

The chapter on instruction includes 3 main areas: media skills, instructional methods, and special instructional considerations, such as body language. The media program is the combination of these services and instruction: the system for putting the building's media resources into the hands of the users.

TECHNICAL SERVICES

Cataloging Procedures should be standardized so that the ability to use the system can be transferred to other library media situations. Mastering that system is an important skill in the lifelong learning process. Changing the media center's cataloging system, besides being an almost impossible task, would create a great deal of confusion and ultimately prove a disservice to the users. For instance, using accession numbers rather than the Dewey Decimal Classification may give students an advantage in finding an item in their media center, but it would greatly handicap their use of other libraries.

When a disabling condition totally precludes the use of the standard cataloging system, you may consider adapting a selected part of the catalog. For example, a book catalog of large print books printed in large print is a logical format or, you may determine a need for audiotaping a catalog of the tape collection. Remember, however, that motivating students to become familiar with standard systems will go further toward encouraging their independent and successful usage of print and nonprint media in the future. Pairing of students to use the card catalog may be the best solution when independent usage is not feasible.

Processing Procedures also depend on the unique needs of your school population. Heavy-duty binding and reinforcement might make students with dexterity problems (and you) more comfortable, knowing that a book will stand up under strenuous usage. Laminating can preserve certain materials (e.g., materials used by students with dexterity or drooling problems). Mounting such items as pictures and maps may increase their usage by students who cannot work flat on the table or on the floor.

Processing may necessitate the changing of a packaging format. Bulky, cumbersome, or flimsy packages may hamper some students. Reinforcement, handles on boxes, or special labels may make those materials usable by more students. Loops attached to items to be placed on higher shelves might enable a shorter student or one in a wheelchair to use a pole to get an item down.

Anticipation may be one of the best ways to extend the usage of materials: Reinforce the things that will get strenuous use. Examine items carefully during processing: Substitute more substantial markers for games, mount and laminate game boards, add clearer directions, and/or make suggestions for use so that the new materials will more effectively meet the needs of the audience for whom they are intended. (For maintenance of material and equipment, see Chapter 8, "Equipment.")

CIRCULATION

There are probably more rules and procedures connected with the circulation of materials than with any other service of the media center. Evaluating the media center's circulation system to determine which rules and procedures are really necessary may be the first step in facilitating circulation for all students. How many of the procedures are barriers? Is excessive paperwork required? Could the process for checking out materials be simplified for all? Are there unnecessary limits placed on the use of materials, such as length of time items can be checked out, number of items allowed out at a time, types of materials that can leave the media center and building, or limited times of the day that items can be checked out? Restricted use, while being an inconvenience for some, might be an absolute barrier for others. Weigh the pros and cons of all procedures. Will a student who uses crutches have to carry around an item or make an extra trip to his/her locker because there is no check-out time at the end of the day? Will s/he be able to carry all materials s/he needs? Will s/he decide not to bother at all . . . ?

Check-out systems can be designed to require little help or supervision and to foster independence. Secondary schools might do well to examine the simplified systems often used in lower grades.

Being flexible does not mean bending the rules, but it may mean devising new rules and procedures which are flexible enough to begin with in order to provide good circulation services to all students. A willingness to be flexible should be part of the media staff's commitment to accommodate all users. Procedures should not bar the way.

REFERENCE

Reference work for disabled students requires the same individual approach used with all students. Some students need simple answers, some need directions, some need guidance, or some need demonstration. School media reference involves more than just getting the information to the user. It means helping that user master reference skills. Challenge each individual to make the best use of the reference system within his/her capabilities.

Current trends for educational accountability and fiscal responsibility promote networking and interlibrary loan activities, as well as other cooperative ventures. In light of current trends, the media specialist should recognize the opportunity for tapping other resources to assist in reference services. It is necessary to become better acquainted with additional sources of information such as public libraries, human resources, special libraries, government agencies, museums, and other organizations in order to meet specific student needs. Basic to reference service is the provision of print and nonprint media to help a student locate information on any topic. And, other agencies may easily provide the needed resources when they are not available in the building collection.

Information service implies that the media specialist is available to answer questions posed by a user. The manner in which this service is rendered is crucial in setting the tone for all other service areas. Sensitivity to individual differences is paramount. Your attitude about making yourself available and approachable helps eliminate one of the barriers which prevents questions from being asked.

CONSULTATION

In order to maintain effective services, media specialists must continually seek ways to assess the informational, instructional, and recreational needs of users. Consultation with teachers and students, through formal and informal encounters, is the best way to stay abreast of changing needs and to provide services and materials that are relevant to them. Consider the following:

1. Keep abreast of changing needs regarding curriculum requirements, new resources, interest trends, new students and/or teachers, educational techniques and theory innovation, availability of new equipment, and self-esteem needs of disabled students.

2. Provide relevant services, such as expanded networking within and outside building, new inservice workshops, additional orientation, orientation to new materials, activities based on transitory needs, and make selection priorities.

3. Work with teachers and other team members on instructional design—"identify student interests and abilities, identify goals and objectives, select appropriate commercial materials, identify teaching methodologies, suggest alternative modes of presenting audiovisual materials, produce materials particularly for these (disabled) students, develop criterion-referenced means of evaluating competencies, and, specify alternative means of evaluating the entire course."[1]

Through consultation with students and staff, media specialists can obtain suggestions for facets of the media program. The purpose of the media program is to serve all possible users and to meet their needs. You may gather this information during informal conversations, via suggestion boxes, and through more formal survey questionnaires. In any case, record the information in a file or notebook as justification for and documentation of changes that are made.

PRODUCTION

A well-equipped and functioning media production center can be a great asset to any media program in attempting to meet the needs of disabled students. The media specialist's primary emphasis should be placed on *designing* materials as part of the school's instructional program, rather than on actual *production*. Special instruction should be scheduled to train teachers, aides, and students in basic production skills. Portions of volunteer or aide programs may include specific responsibilities for production. Facilities, equipment, and supplies for production should be available for use by the entire school.

Production is an essential resource in serving special students. At times, minor modifications may make an item usable by disabled students and their teachers. Other times, the whole format may need to be changed, such as changing audio to visual or visual to audio. It is important to be aware of copyright laws in making modifications and reproducing materials. (See "Copyright Considerations" at the end of Chapter 7.)

A simple production technique is to type ditto masters in large print ("primary" type). Whenever possible, photocopy handouts for students with vision problems instead of giving them ditto copies, because purple ink on white background is one of the hardest color combinations to read. Ditto the rest for cost efficiency. Consider changing the ink color on dittos for all students.

Part of the selection process for new materials is to identify items that meet not only content needs, but also format considerations. For materials that are not commercially available in the format you need, or which cannot be purchased for various reasons, an alternative is to design and produce your own materials. You can produce special units, individual learning packets, practice exercises, supplementary lessons, etc.

If your school has videotape equipment, you have an excellent opportunity to tape the many commercial and educational television specials concerning disabled people. While these programs vary in quality, they often depict disabled people in social and career situations which help to eliminate stereotypes and to provide role models for students. When such programing is negative and biased in depicting disabled persons, it can be used as a basis for clarifying issues and expressing feelings. While it might seem a waste of time to tape and view a blatantly biased production, be aware that these programs are watched and can reinforce attitudinal barriers. It is often better to confront, rather than ignore the issue.

PUBLIC RELATIONS

The media specialist has a major part to play in communicating the media center image to the community and the school. Giving the media program constant visibility in the school and community fosters interest, participation, and support.

Begin by keeping the school informed about what is happening in the media center, particularly those activities which enhance and promote your philosophy of service for the entire school community. Establish a system for getting the word out. Feature, in the school newspaper, news about special activities and the arrival of new equipment and materials. Send out flyers and post announcements around the school about upcoming media events. Consider a monthly newsletter (preferably a student production) to highlight events and services in the media center. Regular announcements to teachers will help keep them abreast of what is going on.

Give open houses in the media center whenever you make changes, obtain items of special interest, or have displays you want to call attention to. A half-hour coffee or tea can provide a relaxed atmosphere for establishing the media center as a pleasant place to be. Focusing on a new idea, materials, or equipment may give a teacher an insight for working with a particular disabled student.

Displays and bulletin boards in the media center and throughout the school can highlight new materials and equipment. They also convey your media and mainstreaming philosophy. At times such displays can feature disabled people, but handle this with a great deal of sensitivity. At all times remember that approximately 13 percent of the population is composed of persons with some form of "exceptionality."[2] Just as you will attempt to depict women, older people and other minorities in regular social situations, so must you also include disabled persons.

Make sure that you carry out your mainstreaming philosophy in the format of your displays. Do not only make displays for people with 20-20 vision. Lettering should be large and easy to read. (Use large letters on a light background; black on yellow is best.) Try raised letters, taped commentary, touchable displays. Be aware of single-concept ideas and color contrast for visual acuity. Keep displays on levels within reach or view of audience.

The community is always monitoring tax dollars and is watching the effects of mainstreaming with interest. Unfortunately there has been much negative publicity on the subject. The media center is a good location not only for open houses for school personnel, but also for community open houses, which give visibility to programs for disabled students. Such an event may allow a concerned parent or citizen to better understand the functioning of the media center and its role in mainstreaming.

Media specialists should take advantage of the many resources available in the community. Community residents are often pleased to help in the media center as volunteers and resource speakers, but few come without being asked. It is the responsibility of the media specialist to inform the community about media programs and activities and to identify persons or groups who have information, skills, or talents which can enhance a media program.

Involve the parents of disabled students in informational forums or informal discussions. Select individuals from the community, particularly parents, disabled persons, or those who work with disabled persons, to serve on an advisory committee for the media center. This committee can be helpful not only for public relations but also for locating resource people in the community.

Setting up a program for bringing disabled persons into your school can "open doors for the 'growing up' dreams of handicapped students, presenting them with real-life models."[3] Contact organizations such as the American Coalition of Citizens with Disabilities and the National Federation of the Blind. The American Association for the Advancement of Science has published a directory of handicapped scientists as part of a role model project. The directory includes 500 handicapped scientists who are willing to speak in schools about education and careers. (See "Selected Resources" section at the end of this chapter.) Such a program can provide nondisabled students with a new perspective of disabled persons and can also assist you and your staff in developing positive attitudes.

Some of the suggestions presented in this section may help lay the foundations for mainstreaming in your school. However, once disabled students are integrated into your programs, do not call adverse attention to their presence by special activities which focus on disabilities.

ORIENTATION

Planning media center orientation programs for students is the responsibility of the media specialist. As with other aspects of media program planning, consult with classroom and special education teachers to ensure that the orientation presentation will be suitable for all students. Avoid orientations designed only for certain students and labeled "special."

Make the orientation flexible by having all components available in varied formats, readily interchangeable. For instance, information can be printed in standard and large type, brailled, photocopied, transferred to transparencies, or tape recorded. Ideally, presentation of the information includes a combination of as many formats as are applicable to the diverse needs of the students attending. Media center guides and handbooks in varied formats can also be made available.

The goal in orientation is to convey all necessary information to all students, while avoiding unnecessary repetition for individuals or groups and the stigmatization of some students requiring "special" attention. Of course, there will be situations where some students will need supplementary orientation. Blind and visually impaired students may need mobility assistance to learn the layout of the center and reorientation if furniture is moved or the environment is changed. Mentally retarded students entering secondary school may have difficulty absorbing the large amounts of information presented in one-time-only orientations. Preparing sound/slide programs and videotaping presentations for repeated playback can help. Approaching orientation as an ongoing, systematic service rather than as an annual event will alleviate this problem.

Many students will need reinforcement of information presented during orientation. Have the information available at all times for individual reference. Observe students and note individual needs for repetition and practice. Provide the assistance individually and informally as part of the everyday service to users. Do not call adverse attention to students needing help by requiring their attendance at additional sessions.

SPECIAL ACTIVITIES

While media specialists may not be able to initiate all of the following activities, they should support their purposes and functions.

Field Trips. Isolation may be a frequent problem for the disabled student. Because special arrangements have often been necessary when transporting students with certain disabilities on field trips, they have often been left out of such activities. Since all public facilities, however (with the exceptions of historical sites), are required by law to be barrier-free, students can have great opportunities for field trip experiences. Media specialists can help teachers select places that will accommodate all their students. Special transportation can be arranged and students can help each other. Field trips are not just frivolous outings. They play an important part in the educational process, and all students should have the opportunity to participate, for their social and academic enrichment.

Guest Speakers. Positive role models for disabled students are often lacking because students seldom see adults functioning successfully in spite of limitations. (Often deaf children assume that when the grow up they will not be deaf because they have never met a deaf adult.) By asking guest speakers who are disabled to come to the media center to speak about their topic of expertise (not their disability), you can provide needed role models for disabled students and help break stereotypes for other students. However, do not discourage students from asking questions about the speaker's disability.

Student Workshops. Presenting student workshops is a service which can cover a variety of interests, needs, and concerns. Design workshops so all can participate. Special topics relating to disabled students may be included as part of a wide range of topics:

- Disability awareness.
- Instruction on use and maintenance of special equipment.
- Production of special materials.
- Instruction on transcribing written material onto tape.
- Instruction on tutoring.
- Exploration of new environments.
- Special skills: sign language, brailling, lipreading.
- Drama: mime, signed theatre, puppetry.
- Biographical sketches of famous disabled persons.
- Poetry and song workshops emphasizing personal feelings.
- Techniques of group interaction and facilitation.
- Sensitivity training.

Storytelling and Booktalks. Feature materials both by and about disabled individuals. Make sure the formats of presentation meet the needs of your audience. For example, a story might be acted out or mimed; it might be illustrated with transparencies, or on a flannel board or through a display.

Other Activities. Encourage student use of the media center through such activities as:

- Contests which stress creativity without emphasizing individual competition, or which allow students to work cooperatively (at paired, group, classroom, or grade levels).
- Contests based on luck or guesswork as opposed to skill mastery, or "everyone's a winner" contests.
- Contests with group rewards, where efforts go for a common cause, such as a "Multiple Sclerosis Read-a-thon," coupon and label collection/redemption programs.
- Media fairs which include materials by, for, and about persons with disabilities.
- Special days, weeks, or months set aside for topical emphasis, such as Blind Awareness Week, or Barriers Awareness Month.
- Birthday recognition of famous disabled persons (emphasizing their achievements, not their disabilities), such as Helen Keller,

Wilma Rudolph, Franklin Delano Roosevelt, Steven Hawking, Thomas Edison. (And, researching and setting up these events would be good student-involvement projects.)

REFERENCES

1. Margaret E. Chisholm and Donald P. Ely, *Media Personnel in Education* (Englewood Cliffs, NJ: Prentice-Hall, Inc., 1976), p. 21.

2. Robert M. Anderson, David H. Martinez, and Rick H. Lindall, "Perspectives for Change," in *Implementing Learning in the Least Restrictive Environment*, ed. John W. Schifani, Robert M. Anderson, Sara S. Odle (Baltimore, MD: University Park Press, 1980, p. 7).

3. Virginia W. Stern and Martha Ross Redden, "Role Models for the Handicapped," *National Elementary Principal* 58 (1) (October, 1978): 43.

SELECTED RESOURCES—SERVICES

Publications

Ruark, Ardis and Carole Melby. *Kangaroo Kapers or How to Jump into Library Services for the Handicapped*. Pierre, SD: Division of Elementary and Secondary Education, 1978.

    A source of information relating to organizations serving the handicapped: lists periodicals, specialized bibliographies, guidelines for the evaluation of educational materials relating to the handicapped, and strategies for effecting change. Designed primarily for use by elementary media specialists.

Terwillegar, Jane, ed. *Special People, Special Needs, Special Services*. Athens, GA: University of Georgia, Department of Educational Media and Librarianship, 1978.

    Gives very practical guidelines relating PL 94-142 to the media specialist. Primarily a reference work with extensive bibliographies, although only some are annotated. Includes checklists, directories, and evaluation and selection criteria. (This report is currently available through the ERIC system, number ED 157 500.)

Velleman, Ruth A. *Serving Physically Disabled People*. New York: R. R. Bowker Co., 1979.

    Explores the informational needs of physically disabled people (mentally and emotionally disabled are not included). Helps define the role of librarians in school, college, and public libraries in meeting those needs and offers pertinent sources of information. One section is devoted exclusively to school library media centers and is particularly helpful in presenting a core collection for serving disabled students.

Wright, Kieth C. *Library and Information Services for Handicapped Individuals*. Littleton, CO: Libraries Unlimited, Inc., 1979.

Although it emphasizes public libraries rather than school library media centers, provides a valuable resource on library services to the handicapped.

Organizations

American Association for the Advancement of Science, Project on the Handicapped in Science, 1176 Massachusetts Ave., N.W., Washington, DC 20036.

The project developed *The Resource Directory of Handicapped Scientists, AAAS Publication No. 78-13*, which is a directory of 500 handicapped scientists who are willing to speak in school about education and careers. They have also developed other materials for teaching science to handicapped students.

Chapter 6
Programs—Instruction

INTRODUCTION

This chapter will deal with 3 aspects of instruction:

1. Skills that should be taught in the media center (including a rationale for the necessity of media skills instruction).
2. Methods that make instruction more relevant to the needs of students with disabilities.
3. Special "instructional considerations" for disabled students which make teaching more effective and, conversely, actions of media specialists/teachers which create barriers to learning.

MEDIA SKILLS INSTRUCTION: CONTENT

Learning basic media skills is an important part of a student's regular school experience. Instruction in these skills is therefore a major component of a quality media program at all levels, grades K–12, and should include disabled students. The skills include locating, using, and communicating information.

More specifically, through a sequential program of media skills instruction, students should acquire the ability to:

1. Identify and locate media or specific contents of media (print and nonprint) after a search.
2. Read, listen to, and view a variety of materials.
3. Locate and select pertinent materials to meet specific needs and specific learning objectives.
4. Select one medium over another, or one part of a material over another part, for some particular learning objective (matching, selecting, distinguishing).

5. Evaluate sources of information, identify authors' intent, and recognize propaganda.
6. Interpret information which requires skills in judging authoritativeness of sources.
7. Utilize, comprehend, and apply information derived from print and nonprint media.
8. Take notes and record sources.
9. Organize information in outline form of sequential arrangement.
10. Select the best medium for summarizing and presenting material.
11. Design and produce media.
12. Present material verbally or pictorially in a clear, concise manner.
13. Communicate ideas effectively.

Disabled students are able to tackle the learning of these skills. Although not all students will reach an advanced level in using these skills, most can reach a functional level. Therefore, every student should be challenged to achieve his/her highest potential. All students need to be taught how to select and process the barrage of information coming at them from all types of print and nonprint media, from books to television.

Teaching these skills throughout the educational process should bring most students to a functional level of media discrimination. This will not happen, however, without a well-designed system of skills instruction in each school. An effective instructional skills continuum for each student and the integration of these skills with relevant curriculum content can best be implemented through the cooperative planning of the classroom teacher and the media specialist.

MEDIA SKILLS SEQUENCE

Whatever media skills sequence you select, it should be designed to reflect a continuum of preschool through high school education in 2 main media-related areas:

- Comprehension-study skills.
- Identification-utilization skills for instructional materials and audio-visual equipment.

If the skill levels do not correspond to grades, but instead represent groupings of skills at developmental stages, students will not be compared with their peers in terms of skill acquisition, but rather viewed at a point along a continuum.

This type of sequence can be used to serve a number of functions, depending on the combined needs of the school's media center, regular classrooms, and the special education program. Three such uses are briefly described: (1) as an assessment tool, (2) as a scope and sequence for instruction, and (3) as a method to assist in the organization of instructional materials.

Assessment. Determination of what skills a student has and does not have is an important prerequisite to a sound instructional program of media skills. Through assessment, a student's strengths and weaknesses are enumerated, and the individual's learning styles and modalities are identified, which leads to more efficient instruction. The special educator, classroom teacher, and media specialist can concentrate on those areas of deficiency. Knowing in what type of environment a student learns best, how to present material (format) and at what rate, and what forms of sensory input/output are most effective, can significantly enhance instruction.

Scope and Sequence for Instruction. An instructional skills continuum is designed to assist in actual instruction. It gives a clear idea of what is next. The determination of what is to be taught is based on the assessment. Once students have demonstrated mastery of a given skill, they will move on to the next unmastered skill. Using assessment information, students can be grouped according to their needs (e.g., all students needing to master a specific level of card catalog use can work together, while those learning to operate a 16mm projector can form another group).

Methods for recording data are individual, varying with the media specialist's training, program needs, and personal teaching styles. Media specialists need to select or develop forms that meet their particular needs.

Organization of Instructional Materials. Learning centers provide an excellent method for managing instruction. Centers can be developed with all types of students in mind, accommodating a wide range of ages, interests, and abilities, and bringing together the materials, equipment, and supplies needed to master particular skills. Efficient organization promotes student independence and allows teachers to spend their time with students, rather than materials.

METHODS

Mediating instruction for all students, that is, matching the most appropriate print and nonprint materials to a student's educational needs, is based on an understanding of the theories and principles of learning. The type of mediation used in a teaching/learning situation is based on a student's needs, learning styles, and strengths. Improper mediation can be worse than none at all:

> . . . while the mediation is aesthetically very pleasing, if not exciting, and while it is quite elaborate and beautiful from a technological point of view, it (may contribute) nothing effective to the teacher-pupil transaction. As a matter of fact, the media may very well get in the way of and detract from the effectiveness of the lesson.[1]

But proper mediation enhances learning and may be the vehicle through which learning takes place. Selecting and developing media are covered more fully in Chapter 7, ''The Media Collection.''

The following methods of instruction may be effective for both disabled and nondisabled students.

Task Analysis

Task analysis is the process of dividing skills into incremental steps to identify the logically ordered components of a particular skill and to aid in pinpointing an obstacle which may be preventing a student from mastering that skill.

Example: Student is able to find a single-word topic in a book by using the book's index.

1. Student opens book.
2. Student locates index in book.
3. Student learns organization of index and directions for use.
4. Student locates index page in alphabetical range of topic.
5. Student locates initial letter of topic.
6. Student locates second letter of topic, etc.
7. Student locates topic.
8. Student locates page number where topic is discussed.
9. Student turns to page where topic is discussed.
10. Student locates topic on page.

The task analysis method can be used in 3 basic ways:

1. The student attempts the task while an observer monitors progress. When the observer pinpoints a problem, the student is given further instruction and practice.
2. The student performs the first step of a task. The instructor then completes the task, explaining each step to the student. The student then performs the first 2 steps and so forth, adding a step each time the instructor works through the task.

3. The instructor explains and completes each step of a task allowing the student to complete the final step. Each time the task is repeated the student completes one more step working backwards. In each case, the student finishes the task and feels a sense of success. (This is called reverse chaining.)

Every media skill does not need to be task-analyzed completely. Be aware that all skills consist of many components. Break down only those areas where students need special help. Through task analysis, you will be able to develop activities for learning each step. Mastering a particular component step (e.g., alphabetizing) will be transferable to mastery of other skills. For more detail on the procedure of task analysis, refer to one of the learning systems design books that are available, such as Cheryl Scanlon's and Patricia Almond's *Task Analysis and Data Collection* (Portland, OR: ASIEP Educational Co., 1981).

Equipment

Media specialists should be aware of the many ways that equipment for presenting audiovisual media can be used by students and teachers in the instructional and learning process. Through equipment, there is access to a multitude of commercial and other productions. Staff and students can produce materials that use available equipment in effective ways.

Standard equipment found in many media centers can be used for many aspects of the teaching-learning process. Audiovisual equipment provides a way, other than print, for the media specialist and other teachers to present information to many students at different times, without repeating the information themselves. Also, information accessed through media equipment can be stored for future use; access is not dependent upon the media specialist's having time to repeat it verbally. Much information (tests, directions, etc.) may already be easily accessible in print formats, but students should have alternatives available for follow-up activities and for future reinforcement.

The following teaching and learning procedures can be accomplished through equipment utilization:

Pretesting. Equipment can be used to determine skill levels and to assess individual student needs. Test materials and instructions can be presented with media equipment; likewise students can give their responses using equipment. For example, a student might view a film and recite answers into a tape recorder. Individualized tests could be given at the same time to several students with little or no teacher participation.

Presentations. A variety of equipment can be used for class presentations. By incorporating a multimedia approach in instruction and presentation of content, the teacher can vastly increase the chances of reaching more students with the information. It is more than just the blind student who needs oral reinforcement, or the deaf student who needs visual examples and explanations. For example, if presentations are mediated, e.g., tape recorded or videotaped, or are presented through films, filmstrips, slides or overhead projector transparencies, the students will be able to refer to the materials as often as necessary to reinforce their learning.

Giving Directions. Through the use of equipment the media specialist can plan, illustrate, or give step-by-step directions. Students can review the directions as often as necessary.

Individualizing Instruction. Not only can the media content be individualized, but the mode of its presentation can be matched to the student's need. Students can work alone, free from distractions.

Group Instruction. Small or large groups can gain information through various types of audio and/or visual presentations.

Monitoring. Students can monitor themselves or provide data for teacher-monitoring of their work. Their errors need not stigmatize them.

Practicing. Students can work at their own pace, reviewing the instructions and/or the content over and over again. They can have immediate feedback on their progress.

Testing. Students can take their time to review, correcting their own work before being evaluated by others.

Equipment can never replace the personality and warmth of the media specialist and staff. Always weigh the advantages of using equipment against the student's need for personal contact and reinforcement; and also consider using media equipment to free the media specialist for working directly with students.

Group Structures

While individualized instruction is a key to meeting the specific needs of students, a balance of individual and group work must be maintained. Isolating a student from group activities can be just as detrimental as isolation in a special classroom. The interaction of disabled and nondisabled students is an essential ingredient of mainstreaming. This interaction should not focus on competition, but rather on cooperation.

> When teachers have students compete with each other to see who is best, students are placed in a situation in which their success determines other students' failure and vice versa. In such a "if I win, you lose; if you win, I lose," situation, differences in performance are viewed negatively. If another student is different in a way that gives him or her a competitive advantage, the difference tends to be feared; if another student is different in a way that places him or her at a

competitive disadvantage, the difference tends to be held in contempt. Thus, competition tends to create further rejection and stigmatization of low performing students, no matter if the low performance is based on physical, intellectual, emotional, or other sorts of differences. For mainstreaming, therefore, competition is out of the question as it promotes the rejection of low performing students as "losers."[2]

The following group structures promote cooperation.

Pairing

1. Pair students who have a common need in skill development. They can be given instruction jointly and can work together on problem solutions. They can quiz each other and monitor work while receiving reinforcement in an area in which they need practice.

2. Pair a student who has a strength with a student who is deficient in the same area. Let them work on a common task emphasizing both cooperation and individual responsibilities for accomplishing specific aspects of the task.

3. Pair students with a common strength to work on a project. Again, emphasis should be placed on cooperation. This type of pairing can contribute to self-esteem since it is success-structured.

Small Cooperative Groups

Johnson and Johnson suggest that a good working group includes 2 average achievers, one high achiever, and one low achiever.[3] Students can be taught facilitation skills so that the group can work independently. Cooperation is learned because the success of the group is dependent upon the achievement of all group members. Students may naturally assume certain roles within the group; however, the media specialist should intervene if some students always fall into the same roles (especially roles which perpetuate stereotypes: for example, girl always records, or boy leads, or retarded student does all the footwork). Or tasks can be assigned to students, such as recording information, checking for accuracy, facilitating the interaction, observing and making suggestions for improving interaction, operating equipment, collecting materials, typing, presenting findings, illustrating ideas (e.g., pointing to words, illustrations, maps).

Large Groups

Working in large groups can help students learn social skills, behavioral requirements, democratic processes, and acceptance of responsibility for their own actions. Individuals are not the center of attention in a large group. Students must learn to pay attention and to respond even when the interaction is not directed specifically at each of them. Cooperation and consideration for others are significant aspects of large group activities. Some disabled students, who spend a good deal of time in individual settings, need large group interaction.

Tutoring

Tutoring is a pairing or a small group situation where one student is assigned the specific role of assisting others to master a task. The students who act as tutors must be trained, not only in teaching techniques, but also in sensitivity. (Include them in the awareness activities discussed in Chapter 4, "Staff Roles.") The media specialist should monitor the interaction on a regular basis and regroup students when negative observations are made. Tutors are not teachers. The media specialist should present new material and use tutors only to reinforce learning. Tutoring should not be used without a clear understanding by the media specialist of the needs of the students to be tutored.

Tutoring in itself is a learning experience for the tutors. Almost all students have some strengths that qualify them to be tutors. The job should not always fall to the highest achieving students, nor should those students be constantly expected to fill that role. Students can be assigned across grade levels, but be aware of the self-esteem of the older student being tutored by a younger student. "One of the most important resources within the school is peers who will encourage educational aspirations, achievement, and appropriate social behavior."[4]

Changing Media Formats

Most students gather information through all of their senses. Disabled students, because of impairments, may be weaker or totally lacking in one or more of their sensory functions. Varying instructional media formats will be essential for those students and will strengthen learning for all students. Examples of varied media formats are: illustrations, flannel boards, overhead transparencies, posters, maps, realia, models, slides, tape recordings and records, filmstrips, motion pictures, and printed materials.

Your instructional methods can be dynamic responses to the varying needs of your students as you grow in new approaches. A static approach to instruction may benefit only one portion of your audience and exclude others. (See Chapter 8, "Equipment," for further examples.)

INSTRUCTIONAL CONSIDERATIONS

The following is a list of instructional considerations. They apply to all students, but it should always be stressed that an action which only enhances learning for a nondisabled student may be essential for the learning of a disabled student. In the same way, an action which detracts from learning for one student may preclude learning for another.

Noise

Some states have official noise standards for public schools. Check to see if your state is one of them. For a number of reasons, including but not limited to hearing impairments, background noises can detract from learning (for example, students with vision problems who depend more on their hearing may be bothered, or students with learning disabilities may be more easily distracted). Just because some may be able to block out distracting sounds, do not assume everyone can. Set up test situations to assess the needs of students and the tolerance they might have for working with noise distractions. You may need to find quieter areas for activities. Consider including background music or ambient noise systems as possible distractors. However, while the music or ambient noise system may muffle out background noise for some students; for others, it may be worse than the noise it is intended to cover.

Body Language

Body language is a means of communication. One need not be an expert to grasp its significance. Observe the way people hold and move their bodies in relation to you and how you react to their actions. Chances are that the kinds of postures which make you feel uncomfortable will also make others uncomfortable. Become aware of what you are saying to others by your body language. Anyone can recognize an approving gesture, when warmth and openness are being projected, just as anyone can ascertain disapproval in nonverbal communication. Disabled persons will recognize uneasiness, impatience, reluctance, and rejection through body language.

Eye contact is part of body language. While there are sometimes cultural considerations to be made (for example, in some cultures looking an elder in the eye is considered rude), looking at a person generally indicates that you are directing attention toward him/her. Giving such attention, both as a speaker and as a listener, is important in helping students to develop self-esteem. Watching a student's eyes is a good way to tell if your message is being received and to detect a student's discomfort or a questioning look. When relating to people who are shorter or seated (for example, wheelchair users), eye contact might necessitate changing your level to meet theirs. And, if you remain standing when talking to a wheelchair-bound student for more than a few minutes, it will be uncomfortable for the student to keep looking up.

Voice

A little effort and thought given to the tone and quality of one's voice will improve instruction for many students. People are often careless in their speech: speaking too fast, too softly, slurring words, fading out at the end of sentences. Improving your enunciation and projection may help you gain and hold the attention of students who ordinarily miss many of your words. Remember how you feel at meetings when the speaker, for various reasons, is unintelligible.

While you are speaking, it is also important to be aware of words themselves. Ask yourself:

- Is your choice of vocabulary appropriate for the students you are addressing?
- Do you define difficult words?
- Do you use unusual phrases without clarification?
- How long are your sentences?
- How many directions do you give?
- Do your word choices reflect biases?
- Do you label people?
- Do your descriptions present a true picture of things some students may never see?

Consider where you stand or sit in relation to the students you are teaching. Being in front of a bright window can virtually blur you out of the picture. If activities are going on behind you, this may be distracting; a bulletin board or pictures not related to your activity can also distract. How close do you sit or stand to the students? Do you cast shadows on their work? Are you too far away for students to read your lips or your facial expressions, or so close that you inhibit free movement and response? Do you move around so much that it might be difficult for some to follow you?

One way of evaluating your teaching style is to have yourself videotaped while giving a lesson. Watching yourself allows you to evaluate your voice and body language and also permits you to see how different students react to your style.

REFERENCES

1. Herbert Goldstein, ''The Role of Media Services in the Education of the Special Student,'' *Issues in Media Management* (1977): 43.

2. David W. Johnson and Robert T. Johnson, *Learning Together and Alone: Cooperation, Competition and Individualization* (Minneapolis, MN: University of Minnesota, 1978), p. 5.

3. Johnson and Johnson, p. 86.

4. Johnson and Johnson, pp. 37–38.

SELECTED RESOURCES—INSTRUCTION

Publications

Haring, Norris G., and Schiefelbusch, R. L. *Teaching Special Children.* New York: McGraw-Hill Book Co., 1967.

> Presents a number of instructional models in summarized form and also discusses complete instructional packages.

Stephens, Thomas M.; Hartman, A. Carol; and Lucas, Virginia H. *Teaching Children Basic Skills: A Curriculum Handbook.* Columbus, OH: Charles E. Merrill Publishing Co., 1979.

> Contains over 700 "short-term objectives" required as part of IEPs, sample assessment tactics and teaching activities, and exercises in creating assessment tactics and teaching activities.

Thomas, M. Angele, ed. *Developing Skills in Severely and Profoundly Handicapped Children.* Reston, VA: Council for Exceptional Children, 1977.

> A product of the Educational Resources Information Center (ERIC) Clearinghouse on Handicapped and Gifted Children; presents 10 outstanding articles.

Organizations

Center for Innovation in Teaching the Handicapped (CITH), Indiana University, 2085 E. 10th St., Bloomington, IN 47401.

> CITH's current major objective is to design, develop, and disseminate high priority teacher training materials and innovative training systems. Send for brochures, pamphlets, and fact sheets.

Chapter 7
The Media Collection

INTRODUCTION

This chapter summarizes steps for developing a media collection which is responsive to the needs of disabled students. Methods and strategies are delineated for determining what materials are available in the media center, the school, and the district support systems which can be used by and for disabled students; for strengthening the procedures for the evaluation and selection of materials and equipment; for developing a collection which meets the needs of disabled students; and for identifying sources for borrowing and funding of specialized materials and equipment for disabled students.

INVENTORY

Knowledge of the content of the media collection is a prerequisite for its effective use. In meeting the needs of disabled students, the first step is to inventory the media center collection. Focus on identifying all materials, print and nonprint, that can potentially be used by and for disabled students and by teachers and others interested in their needs.

Another step is to collect, catalog, and inventory all materials from around the school which have not previously been part of the media center collection. Check classrooms, special education resource rooms, and teacher collections for such materials. Ask the cooperation of all teachers in this aspect of the inventory process. You may find that many of them prefer materials to be centrally organized, cataloged, housed, and administered from the media center. Many will welcome the added space the process will leave on their classroom shelves and bookcases. Explain to teachers who are reluctant to part with materials that you are taking an inventory and developing a more complete catalog of the school's holdings to include materials for disabled students in order to be of better service. Teachers wanting materials for classroom use can check them out on a short- or long-term basis after they have been processed. There are many advantages to developing a central catalog which lists all materials in the entire school. You, as well as faculty, students, and others will also have access to the information. The central catalog can save money by eliminating unplanned duplicate purchasing. Further, material that has not previously been used may be brought to the attention of a potential user.

The third step in the inventory process is to note what existing media formats are available through the collection. It can be advantageous to discover, for example, that a required novel or short story is available in several different formats such as books, tape recordings, or motion pictures, so that students having difficulty in reading or who digest information more easily from nonprint formats can be accommodated.

The fourth step is to identify those catalogs which list materials available through the school district and local educational service district. Ultimately, you are trying to assess the strengths and weaknesses of the media center collection and what you might need to purchase or borrow in order to enhance that collection. Unless an item is in constant demand, its availability through district channels may satisfy your school's needs.

NEEDS ASSESSMENT

Knowing *what* is in the collection is only the first step. Determining the usefulness of the collection is next and involves 2 steps: (1) assessing student needs and (2) evaluating the collection in terms of those needs.

Student needs will be affected by their learning style. Everyone learns differently. Fortunately (given the tradition of schools), many people can learn from formats not necessarily best suited to them. For example, many students can understand oral instructions, even when written instructions might be more effective. But if some impairment should limit one or more sensory functions, it becomes crucial that other formats be used. Whenever possible, the same information should be available in a number of formats so that the student can respond to the material best suited to his/her learning style. The various formats will also reinforce information gained in other ways.

The most effective media for the disabled student is frequently the most effective media for all students. The principles for selecting the most effective media remain the same unless a specific need precludes the use of that media. Remember, however, that while quality of presentation may add or detract from an item's effectiveness with a nondisabled student, it may totally preclude usage by a student who is in some way impaired. One student may be able to determine what the visual presentation or word or sound is, while for another student it is totally lost.

Some general criteria for determining quality follow:

1. It is beneficial for all students to have materials prepared with quality print on quality paper stock. The concern is for optimal legibility, regardless of artistic format or cost.
   a. Light colored or white nonreflective paper should be used.
   b. Print shadows should not be visible from the back side.
   c. Print should be clear with separation between letters and lines; it should be smudge-free.
   d. Print should be separated from pictures or collage backgrounds.

2. Legibility considerations should also apply to film, transparencies, graphics, posters, maps, globes, and other media. It is essential that there is a clear presentation of concepts. Several concepts together may be distracting and may deter learning, except where comparison is the objective. Overlays may be used effectively when presenting more than one concept. Captions should not be placed over irregular backgrounds.

3. Intelligibility is essential with all auditory media. Cassette tapes, records, and sound tracks need to be produced in clear, intelligible voices. Use of standard, unaccented English is usually best. Where content is carried by dialect, as in some narratives, use supplementary scripts or discussion.

4. Durability is an essential quality to look for in evaluating games, toys, models, sculpture, and specimens. Learning is more comfortable for the student who does not share the media specialist's anxiety over the replacement cost of some fragile item.

Consult Chapters 10–16 in Part 3, "Specific Disabling Conditions for Students," for special collection considerations.

The media collection should relate to the interests of all students. Disabled students have interests as varied as other students, making access to the general collection essential.

One area of interest to most students is career awareness. Materials should be provided which show disabled persons in traditional jobs and professions. Watch your biases. Disabled persons can and do work in nearly every kind of job. Showing them in a wide variety of roles helps dispel prejudices and encourages disabled students to broaden options in career planning. Contact your state vocational rehabilitation department and the President's Committee on Employment of the Handicapped for career materials. (See "Selected Resources" section at the end of this chapter.)

The media collection supports and supplements the classroom. Being aware of what is going on in the classroom and serving on curriculum and instruction committees enables the media specialist to relate the collection to current classroom needs. Special materials may be needed for specific skill levels and skill development. Work closely with the teacher and student in selecting these materials. While materials may be purchased with disabled users in mind, no item should be set aside exclusively for their use. This stigmatizes the material and its user and limits the benefit of its use by any student who might need work in a special area.

The self-esteem of students is enhanced when they see themselves in the materials they use. If disabled students only see characters without disabilities or only see disabled persons depicted in either disparaging or idealized ways, their self-esteem is lowered. This is no different from girls seeing no positive, realistic images of women, or minorities seeing only white faces.

The Council for Exceptional Children (CEC) has compiled a list called "Guidelines for the Representation of Exceptional Persons in Educational Media," which can be used in determining whether your media collection fosters a "positive, fair and balanced representation of exceptional persons in print and nonprint educational materials."[1] These guidelines include concern for adequate representation of disabled persons on a percentage basis, representation in all types of materials at all levels, accurate representation free of stereotypes, and so forth.

Students may come to the media center specifically in search of information about certain disabling conditions. It is important that the media specialist have accurate information available or know where to direct students for more details. Other students may take an interest in a topic because the material is available.

EVALUATION OF EXISTING CONDITIONS

Once you are aware of what is in the school's media collection and have ascertained the specific needs of the disabled students in your school, you can develop methods and strategies for evaluation.

Start by reviewing your written selection policy. The selection of quality instructional materials and equipment is one of the most important tasks performed by the media specialist and other school personnel. The selection policy should provide the basis for developing and maintaining excellent quality in the materials used for teaching and learning. Remember that it is the responsibility of the media center to provide a wide range of materials on different levels of difficulty, with diversity of appeal, and representing different points of view. Does your selection policy contain guidelines for selecting materials to meet the needs of disabled students in your school? Does it contain guidelines that ensure a variety of media formats? Does it specify requirements for clarity, intelligibility of language, fair representation of disabled persons, etc.? Does it provide for continuous evaluation of the collection to account for emerging needs? A well-written selection policy will guide you and others in selecting materials for use by and for disabled students.

Involve others in the evaluation of materials—students, teachers, parents and resource persons outside the school—they each have a unique perspective. A disabled student may be the best judge of the utility of an item. These individuals may also have insights on how to make items useful through minor adaptations.

It is important to have administrative support. Keep the school administration aware of what you have discovered—what materials are available, what the media needs of disabled students are. Keep records of usage to show why you need more copies or more materials in certain content areas. Keep a consideration file with reviews of materials you would like to purchase when money becomes available. Be able to justify those needs.

STRENGTHENING THE COLLECTION

Based upon your inventory, the needs assessment of your school, and a careful evaluation of the material, you will be able to identify the gaps in your collection. Before you buy, check out the possibilities for borrowing. You may have a student with a specific disability who will be in your school for only a short period of time. Could highly specific material be borrowed for that time period? (For example, the American Foundation for the Blind has specific materials it will lend to students officially identified by the Foundation.) Perhaps students will be dealing with a topic for a short time, and material is only needed for a unit. Or, your budget may not be able to support a costly item at this time. Perhaps you are considering a purchase but would like to try the material first. Maybe another center close at hand has what you need and would be willing to share in exchange for something you use less frequently. Start with local libraries, universities, and foundations concerned with specific disability conditions. Consult the state library and the Library of Congress—National Library Service for the Blind and Physically Handicapped (NLS).

New materials can sometimes be developed to meet the needs of disabled students. Pictures can be added to sound presentations, films can be captioned, print can be recorded. If you have a production staff, they can develop materials. Students can also become involved in projects, such as retelling the story from a film so that it is meaningful to someone just listening and not viewing, or by expressing in words the feelings of a musical selection.

When purchases must be made, check into funding sources outside your school. Service clubs, churches, and foundations often have money available for special projects. You might be asked to give a presentation or write up a justification for your need, but at this stage you should have all the support criteria required.

Much material is now being marketed for use in mainstreaming. Write to various educational publishers requesting catalogs of new materials specifically aimed at mainstreaming. Carefully examine materials for mainstreaming to make sure that new labels haven't just been added to old products. While this might show that regular materials can be used with disabled students, you might end up paying a higher price for "specialized material" or duplicate something your collection already contains. Whenever possible preview material before you buy, and try it with the students and teachers. Four things to watch for, according to Gordon Bleil in the article "Evaluating Educational Materials" *(Journal of Learning Disabilities,* January 1975),[2] are:

1. *Magic Solutions*. Ask publishers if they will guarantee results with the students, or if they have substantiations for any claims made in promoting their products.

2. *Diagnostic Labels*. Labels may or may not accurately indicate students for whom materials are appropriate. Putting a diagnostic label on materials is a marketing strategy. Ask for substantiation.

3. *Fad Words or Phrases*. Jargon, such as "high interest, low vocabulary," develops in every field of human endeavor. If used as a convenient shorthand to facilitate understanding, it can be useful. But jargon can be popularized and can cause the same problems that diagnostic lables do: It implies a matching of materials to a need, which may or may not be accurate or necessary.

4. *Grade Levels*. Find out who picked the level and whether you can rely on it. This is particularly important in dealing with students who already have learning problems.

COLLECTION CONTENT

While today's media centers combine print and nonprint collections, media specialists know that the literary quality of materials is still of great importance. Materials must always be selected with a view toward literary excellence; they should relate to and expand the world of the disabled student.

There are many claims made for the affect good literature can have on young people. Many people can recall a book or movie that changed their life views, many believe that books can themselves serve as therapy (bibliotherapy) in helping people overcome certain problems. Literature can have positive effects, particularly in helping students develop self-esteem and expand their life views. But there are no "magic" books which will overcome an emotional problem, cure a learning disability, or make a blind student see. Good quality literary materials should be available for *all* students and the selection of such materials should be made with the needs of *all* students in mind.

COPYRIGHT CONSIDERATIONS

Become familiar with the copyright law, effective since January 1, 1978. A copy of the law is available free of charge by writing to the Copyright Office, Library of Congress, Washington, DC 20559. When you write, ask to have your name added to the Copyright Office mailing list in order to stay current with changes and interpretations of the regulations.

1. Know what is considered "fair use" and when it is necessary to request permission to copy or change material:
   a. Request permission if the use for which you intend it is not covered by the concept of "fair use."
   b. Request permission if changing the media format (i.e., making slides from pictures in a book).
   c. Request permission if changing the media by adding or subtracting elements (i.e., adding captions to a filmstrip, cutting out sections of a film).
2. Know whom to ask permission from: Send a self-addressed stamped business envelope for a free copy of the *Directory of Rights and Permissions Officers* from: Association of Media Producers, 1707 L St., Suite 515, Washington, DC 20036.
3. Know what to do:
   a. Call or write the media producing company explaining clearly what you specifically propose to do to the materials, how they will be used, and the duration and extent of their usage.
   b. Inquire about fees and special considerations.

    c. Send a form which states your specific request and gives the company a place to give signed permission to use media in the way you propose.

    d. Keep copies of all your correspondence and the authorization from the company in your files.

SUMMARY

1. Take an inventory to find out what resources are available in your school: the media collection, special education resource rooms, teacher and classroom collections. Organize a central catalog so everyone will have access to the material and equipment.
2. Know what resources outside the building are readily available: district collections or regional educational service district collections.
3. Assess the needs of the disabled students you serve and the needs of others who serve them.
4. Evaluate your collection according to those needs.
5. Review and revise your selection policy to include guidelines for selecting materials to meet the needs of disabled students.
6. Strengthen your collection.
    a. Weed out poor material.
    b. Try to adapt what you have.
    c. Borrow when possible.
    d. Develop new material.
    e. Purchase new material using stringent selection criteria, previewing when possible.
    f. Investigate additional funding sources.
    g. Let your needs be known.
7. Select all materials—for disabled, as well as nondisabled, students—with a view toward literary excellence.
8. Know the copyright law.

REFERENCES

1. Council for Exceptional Children, *Guidelines for Representation of Exceptional Persons in Educational Media*. Reston, VA: Council for Exceptional Children—Publications, 1979.

2. Gordon Bleil, "Evaluating Educational Materials," *Journal of Learning Disabilities* 8 (1) (January 1975): 12–19.

SELECTED RESOURCES—THE MEDIA COLLECTION

Publications

Baskin, Barbara H., and Harris, Karen H. *Notes from a Different Drummer: A Guide to Juvenile Fiction Portraying the Handicapped.* New York: R. R. Bowker Co., 1977.

Gives rationale for evaluating books on handicaps, plus short annotations and analyses of 300 books. An excellent book.

Bibliography of Secondary Materials for Teaching Handicapped Students. Washington, DC: President's Committee on Employment of the Handicapped, 1977.

Lists materials dealing with the delivery of special education, vocational education, and industrial arts services to handicapped individuals.

Dreyer, Sharon Spredermann. *The Bookfinder.* Circle Pines, MN: American Guidance Service, 1977.

A guide to children's literature about the needs and problems of youth, ages 2–15; describes and categorizes 1,031 children's books according to more than 450 psychological, behavioral, and developmental topics of concern to youth.

Guidelines for the Representation of Exceptional Persons in Educational Media. Reston, VA: Council for Exceptional Children, 1979.

Provides guidelines to evaluate the media center collection.

NICEM Index to Non-Print Special Education Materials—Multimedia. 2 volumes. Los Angeles: National Information Center for Educational Materials (NICEM) and National Information Center for Special Education Materials (NICSEM), 1979.

Includes 2 separate volumes: the *Learner volume* contains 35,558 titles and abstracts on materials suitable for direct instruction of the handicapped; the *Professional Volume* contains 5,192 abstracts of media and materials selected for use by parents of exceptional children, special education teachers, and other professionals.

Pick a Title. Baltimore, MD: The Maryland State Department of Education, 1978.

A bibliographic collection of children's books and other media about the handicapped; provides short annotations.

Sadker, Myra Pollack and Sadker, David Miller. *Now Upon a Time.* New York: Harper and Row, 1977.

A reference work about children's books with a good section on handicaps and children. Includes annotated bibliographies.

Organizations

Handicapped Learner Materials Distribution Center, Indiana University, Audio-Visual Center, Bloomington, IN 47405.

> Send for *Catalog of Instructional Materials for the Handicapped Learner*. Materials in this catalog are available on free loan (excepting return postage) for 1–7 day periods. Items are loaned for preview purposes and actual usage with handicapped persons, but only if the items are not available from local media resource centers.

National Center of Educational Materials for the Handicapped (NCEMMH).

> See end of Chapter 4: "Selected Resources—Staffing; Organizations" for citation.

National Information Center for Special Education Materials (NICSEM).

> See end of Chapter 4: "Selected Resources—Staffing; Organizations" for citation.

The President's Committee on Employment of the Handicapped, Department of Labor, 1111 20th St., N.W., Washington, DC 20210.

> A nationwide program to employ handicapped workers; send for free publication, *Disabled USA*, which presents new promotional and educational activities. Inquire about career education materials.

Teaching Resources Corporation, 100 Boylston St., Boston, MA 02116.

> Send for free catalog which provides detailed descriptions of over 200 programs and materials for special education, early childhood, and language development. Company publishes a series of 15 books, "TR's Mainstreaming Series," designed to help teachers and specialists understand and work with exceptional children.

Materials for Developing Student Awareness

AID: Accepting Individual Differences. Developmental Learning Materials, 7440 Natchez Ave., Niles, IL 60648.

> A kit designed to help elementary and middle-grade students learn to understand, accept and develop positive attitudes to people with handicaps. Kit contains 4 large picture books, 5 teacher's guide booklets, and 1 cassette.   E-M

Aiello, Barbara. *The Invisible Children*. Learning Corporation, 1350 Avenue of the Americas, New York, NY 10019.

> A film (also available in videocassette) designed to encourage children to understand and accept their disabled peers. Stars the innovative puppet troupe "The Kids on the Block."   E-M

Code: E—Elementary, M—Middle, J—Junior High, S—Senior High, GA—General Audience

Berger, Gilda. *Learning Disabilities and Handicaps*. New York: Watts, 1978.

A book dealing with the attitudes of young people toward the physically impaired and defining most of the specific impairments. It examines the history of disabilities, their treatment, and provides scientific information and current available treatment.   J-S

Better Understanding of Disabled Youth (BUDY) (1980). Ideal School Supply, 11000 S. Lavergne Ave., Oak Lawn, IL 60453.

A series consisting of 5 units of multimedia kits which provide teachers and elementary school children with needed information. Also provides a variety of activities for improving understanding of human differences in order to achieve interaction and integration. Each BUDY unit contains a teacher's manual, a filmstrip and audio cassette, a poster, stories, and student manipulatives and/or worksheets.   E

Family Relations. Vision, Hearing, and Speech Series (1972). Creative Arts, 2323 4th St., N.E., Washington, DC 20002.

Six 9″ × 11″ prepared transparencies. Each transparency presents symptoms of specific impairment.   M

Feeling Free. Englewood Cliffs, NJ: Scholastic Books, 1979.

Six 16mm films (also available in video format), activities, and storybooks. Designed for use in grades 4–6, the materials help students to better understand handicapping conditions by presenting children who have different handicaps, in their homes and schools. Materials are sensitively prepared and informative.   M

Films Incorporated. 733 Green Bay Rd., Wilamette, IL 60091.

A company which has produced a number of film series, some from the "Zoom" television series, and which provide positive images of handicapped young people. Send for catalog *Exceptional Films about Exceptional Children*.   M-J

Haskins, James. *Who Are the Handicapped?* NY: Doubleday, 1978.

Excellent book for junior high age and up to help develop positive feelings toward disabled people.   J

I'm Just Like You (1977). Sunburst Communications, Victoria Production, Inc., 39 Washington Ave., Pleasantville, NY 10570.

Two filmstrips, 2 cassettes, and a teacher's guide. Materials are about a 13-year-old blind boy who adequately copes with his disability. General audience appeal.   M

Kids Come in Special Flavors. Box 562, Dayton, OH 45405.

A kit containing complete, ready-to-use teaching materials and simple instructions to simulate the actual inconvenience of being handicapped. Exercises help kids, grades 3–12, explore physical and psychological stum-

---

Code: E—Elementary, M—Middle, J—Junior High, S—Senior High, GA—General Audience.

bling blocks created by disabilities. Includes 15 simulations, questions for discussion, cassette tape, guide book.   GA

Matthew and Julie and the Spanish Dancer. White Plains, NY: National Foundation/March of Dimes, 1975.

This filmstrip kit features 2 filmstrips about a 9-year-old girl born without arms or legs. In *Julie*, she and her teenage siblings share their observations concerning her reception into a society where disabled people are a minority. *Spanish Dancer* is filmed in a documentary style and is an informative and optimistic sequel to *Julie*. *Matthew* features a multiply disabled boy. General audience appeal.   GA

Meet Series (1978). H & H Enterprises, Inc., P.O. Box 1070, Lawrence, KS 66044.

A kit containing 4 books and matching records to explain disabling conditions to nondisabled children, preschool through second grade. Titles include *Meet Lance* (trainable mentally retarded), *Meet Danny* (multiply disabled), *Meet Scott* (learning disabled), and *Meet Camille and Danille* (hearing impaired).   E

Mimi: This is Who I Am (1977). Guidance Associates, 757 3rd Ave., New York, NY 10017.

A filmstrip and guide to help viewers (students and adults) gain understanding about the physically disabled. The filmstrip is about and narrated by Mimi Nelkin, including her own thoughts and life experiences. General audience appeal.   GA

People . . . Just Like You (1979). President's Committee on Employment of the Handicapped, Committee on Youth Development, Washington, DC 20210.

An activity guide containing 24 suggested activities to develop understanding and to improve attitudes of students in grades K–12.   GA

Please Know Me As I Am. The Jerry Cleary Co., 25 Ronald Rd., Sudbury, MA 01775.

A guide to help elementary children understand the child with special needs, its format involves teacher application and children's reactions to the concepts presented. Includes 11 curriculum suggestions with course instruction, teacher application, and preparation for eliciting children's reactions.   E

Pursell, Margaret Sanford. *Look at Physical Handicaps*. Minneapolis, MN: Lerner Publishers, 1976.

A book which encourages readers to understand, not pity, those who are impaired. Through black and white photography and a simple text, the problems of people who have physical handicaps are portrayed.   E-M

Code: E—Elementary, M—Middle, J—Junior High, S—Senior High, GA—General Audience.

Put Yourself in My Place (1978). Guidance Associates, Inc., 757 3rd Ave., New York, NY 10017.

A kit containing 2 color filmstrips, 2 cassettes, and discussion guide. The program considers the adolescent dilemma of peer acceptance versus individual identity.   J-S

Teen Scenes (1979). Developmental Learning Materials, 7440 Natchez Ave., Niles, IL 60648.

Twelve full color posters 12″ × 18″. Pictures handicapped students at work and in recreational settings. Instruction sheets provide a variety of discussion questions and background information for each poster subject.   J-S

What If You Couldn't . . . ? A Program About Handicaps (1978). Children's Museum of Boston with WGBH-TV. Burt Harrison and Co., P.O. Box 732, Weston, MA 02193.

A kit whose purpose is to "create an awareness and sensitivity among nondisabled kids and teachers to the needs of handicapped kids." Designed for elementary and middle-school children, includes lesson plans and activities, simulation experiences and problem solving exercises, masters for worksheets and handouts, a book, and pamphlets.   E-M

Code: E—Elementary, M—Middle, J—Junior High, S—Senior High, GA—General Audience.

Chapter 8
Equipment

INTRODUCTION

Equipment is of primary importance in using a multimedia approach to learning. The following chapter describes how the versatility of standard media center equipment can be used to meet the needs of disabled students and the media specialist's responsibility when specialized equipment is needed.

Student's mastery of equipment operation has many benefits:

- Equipment use can build students' self-confidence by allowing them to work independently in noncompetitive situations.
- Programs can be designed so that students can monitor their own success.
- The variety that is possible with presentation of multimedia materials can increase interest in subject areas.
- Student use of equipment frees staff to work personally with other students.

Disabled students will need the same basic kinds of equipment as other students but, if their primary mode of learning is dependent upon a certain piece of equipment, special consideration must be given.

More Frequent Availability. This may entail buying more of the same item or perhaps changing the usage schedule to ensure that students have the equipment they need.

Regular Maintenance. If the need for an item is crucial, it cannot sit broken on a shelf for weeks. Equipment checks must be made regularly to evaluate for proper functioning. High quality of audio and visual presentation is all the more important when one or more of the senses is impaired. Also, be alert for parts which stick or require extra force or manipulation.

Students (including disabled) can be assigned to regularly monitor and check software quality and hardware functioning. Students can also handle simple maintenance procedures, such as cleaning or oiling. Lines of communication should be kept open with repair services and personnel so that when items do break down, the repair time will be minimal.

Access and Mobility. Equipment should be stored in ways that allow students to reach, move, use and manipulate as independently as possible.

It is the responsibility of the media specialist to understand the potential of specific pieces of equipment and how to manipulate them to achieve maximum efficiency. Consider the advantages of automatic-load equipment, which is easier for students to learn to use independently than are manual-load pieces. Cassette tape recorders are less complicated to use than reel-to-reel tape recorders. Also, some equipment brands are easier to understand and manipulate than others.

Media specialists should emphasize the features that facilitate equipment operation when selecting new equipment for purchase and when choosing items in the center for use by specific students. Most importantly, *before assuming that new audiovisual equipment is needed for disabled students, think of how the present equipment can be used and adapted.* Start with the standard equipment in the media center, and consider the features that have potential for enhancing a particular disabled student's learning experiences.

STANDARD EQUIPMENT

Various uses for equipment in instruction are described under the "Methods" section in Chapter 6, "Programs—Instruction." The following list of equipment presents, for each item, those characteristics lending themselves well to special instructional needs. Certain considerations for each piece of equipment are also listed.

Overhead Projectors

- Class can see the instructor's face; eye contact is allowed.
- Speaker, who is facing audience, is easier to hear; students with hearing impairments can read lips and see facial expressions.
- Speaker can encourage enthusiasm by facial expression.
- Black writing on a white background is easier to read than white chalk on a blackboard.
- Information on acetate can be saved for student review.
- Commercially made transparencies are abundantly available in most subject areas.
- Transparencies can be readily prepared by media center aides, teachers, and students.

Cassette Recorders

- Oral presentation helps students having difficulty with reading.
- Reinforcement of oral or written directions is possible and can be repeated as often as necessary.
- Playback allows the student to repeat sections as needed.
- Tapes can easily be made by teachers, students, aides, or volunteers.
- Tapes are easily handled and stored.
- Tapes are cheap and reusable.
- Heavy duty or classroom models are sturdier and control mechanisms are easier to activate than are smaller portables.
- Headphones can be used for amplification.

Filmstrip Projectors and Viewers

- Students can learn to use them; there are few operating steps.
- Students can view them repeatedly.
- They are an inexpensive and audiovisual format.
- Filmstrip without sound can be viewed at varied rates of speed.
- Filmstrip/cassette can be stopped more easily than filmstrip/record.
- Small screen of filmstrip viewer lessens distraction.
- Versatile size of projection is good for both group and independent usage.

16mm Projectors

- Automatic load operation is within most students' abilities to learn.
- A large range of films is available to purchase, borrow, or rent, including captioned films.

Typewriters

- They are useful for students who have difficulty writing.
- Electric typewriters require little strength to operate.
- Large print (primary type) is suitable for students with visual impairments.
- They provide a viable skill for use outside school.
- Practicing is fun.

Video Equipment

- Students can see themselves.
- Students receive immediate feedback.
- Character generating equipment is available for captioning tapes for the hearing impaired.
- Students can learn to operate video equipment.

Headphones*

- Distractions are lessened and concentration is encouraged.
- Audio can be amplified.
- Sets with dual controls have versatility for use with hearing impaired.
- Students are able to use audio equipment without disturbing others.

Cameras

- They provide an easy means of visual communication.
- Self-expression and creativity in communication can be learned.
- Minimal skills are required; there is no need to read or speak.
- Use of cameras which develop pictures on the spot gives students immediate satisfaction.
- Operation of Instamatic-type is easy to teach and learn and easy for students to teach each other.
- Students learn to focus attention on subject.
- They are good media for leading into other skill and subject areas, e.g., photo developing, filmmaking, layout, art, public relations, community awareness, mass communications.

8mm Film Loop Projectors

- They offer a one-step operation; however, some students may need assistance.
- Programs usually feature a single-concept theme or short subject.
- Their format allows for continual review.
- Size of screen projection (large to small) makes them suitable for group as well as for independent use.

---

*Consult with special educators about using headphones in combination with hearing aids.

Magnetic Card Readers

- They are small and portable.
- They are inexpensive.
- Simultaneous presentation of auditory and visual elements is possible.
- Immediate feedback of student performance is given.
- Commercial prerecorded cards are available, as well as blank cards.
- Cards are reusable.

Calculators

- They are easy to learn.
- They are small and easy to handle.
- A variety of models and features are available.
- Many types are inexpensive.
- More elaborate models, called talking calculators, are available for skills other than mathematics.
- Immediate feedback is provided.
- They encourage repeated practice.

Programed Teaching Machines

- Some very expensive models can be leased.
- Immediate feedback is given.
- There are a variety available: many are easy to use and give varied feedback (sound, voice, lights).
- It is easy to learn to use them.
- They encourage repeated practice.
- Their format allows for drill.

Production Equipment (Ditto, Dry Mount, Visual Maker by Kodak)

- Operation is simple; it is easy to learn and easy to teach.
- Creativity is encouraged.
- Quality of teacher/student production is enhanced.

Support Equipment (carts)

- They provide easy storage and transport of heavy and cumbersome equipment.
- Varied heights are available for different purposes.

Besides recognizing the features of equipment that make them well-suited for use with and by disabled students, investigate innovative ways to use the equipment. Usage alternatives or variations may postpone or eliminate the need to purchase new items, as well as liven up the media and instructional programs.

NEW TECHNOLOGY—THE MICROCOMPUTER

The most revolutionary technology on the media horizon is the microcomputer. This new equipment is predicted to have a major impact on media center management, as well as on the teaching and learning process. The microcomputer has special implications for disabled students.

What is a microcomputer? Essentially, it is a small-size system that includes all 4 of the elements of its larger cousin, the computer: "INPUT— MEMORY—(obvious, and the more the better); CENTRAL PROCESSING UNIT— it 'thinks' logically and arithmetically, and faster than a speeding bullet; and OUTPUT—(all you ever wanted to know about . . .)"[1]

All the information fed into a microcomputer is stored either on a cassette or on a "floppy disk." The information contained on the cassette or diskette is called up with the use of a typewriter-type keyboard, and displayed on a built-in screen or separate display unit (television receiver).

> . . . information or commands to the computer are given in one of several computer languages. The one most commonly used in microcomputers is BASIC, an acronym meaning Beginner's All-Purpose Symbolic Instruction Code."[2]

How can microcomputers be used in education?

1. *School and classroom management:* for keeping track of attendance, individual progress of each student, lesson plans, inventories, reporting, etc.
2. *Media center management:* for equipment inventory, materials inventory, bibliographical searching, cataloging operations, lesson plans, reporting, etc.
3. *Instructional programs schoolwide:* for individualized pacing of curriculum, concept learning, real life simulation, practice and drill, etc.

The microcomputer has special significance for all educators who have contact with and responsibility for mainstreamed students. At the administrative level, microcomputers can be used to keep track of data and information such as Individualized Education Programs (IEPs) and data for state and federal government use in assessing school districts' compliance with legislation affecting the education of disabled children and youth.

But, more importantly, *the microcomputer can be a valuable tool for extending the teaching/learning process to mainstreamed disabled students in the media center*. Providing easy access to the computers, making them available to students, even permitting microcomputers to be checked out, can have a tremendous impact when working with disabled students. Some of the positive aspects of computer use are:

- A high interest program is provided.
- Computers are nonthreatening and easy to use.
- The activity or learning concept can be repeated as many times as necessary until the concept is grasped.
- Students can work at their own pace.
- Programs can be tailored to the individual student's needs.
- Peer tutors can be used.
- Immediate feedback is given.
- Lack of negative comments from classmates when wrong response is given to a question improves student's self-confidence.
- Self-proficiency is promoted.
- Responsibility and self-discipline are instilled.
- Growth of self-esteem is seen.[3]

It is perhaps the last item which has the greatest value. When disabled students can go to the media center, just like the other students in the school, and use the newest and most sophisticated electronic equipment to do an assignment, their self-image grows positively and receives reinforcement.

A media specialist does not need to know computer programing methods in order to have microcomputers in the media center. It is necessary, however, to have some knowledge of the equipment in terms of what it can do and how it can help facilitate the learning process for individual students, including mainstreamed disabled students.

EQUIPMENT MODIFICATIONS

You can find ways of modifying equipment that students cannot operate. Modifications may include replacing small switches and knobs with larger ones (such as tennis balls or long levers), eliminating knobs in favor of sensitive push buttons, or covering knobs with coarsely textured material to facilitate grasp and turning. These modifications permit students with limited fine motor control to use gross motor movements instead, and vice versa. For instance, extending the push buttons on a cassette recorder by gluing on longer wood or metal strips makes its operation a hand, arm, or elbow movement rather than a finger movement. This same modification would also benefit the student with limited strength. Try the media center's cassette recorders with this in mind; you may not have realized how hard you have to push to activate the machine, especially to record. Various textures also help the visually impaired student identify knobs for different purposes.

You may or may not feel qualified to make major alterations on your equipment. Everyone, however, can probably cut a hole in a tennis ball to fit over a small knob or attach sandpaper to the acetate roll control on an overhead projector.

When help is needed, there are several sources to turn to. For free assistance, contact audiovisual specialists, industrial arts and electronics teachers, and custodians or maintenance people in your school or district. Students too may be able to help. Resource persons outside the school district may include your regional education service district, state department of education, higher education personnel, the state department of vocational rehabilitation, as well as volunteers from the community.

SPECIALIZED EQUIPMENT

Another alternative to adapting and modifying equipment is developing (or inventing) new equipment, which is an alternative outside the realm of probability for most media specialists. However, new equipment is being developed all the time—someone is doing it!

The Telephone Pioneers of America, an organization of retired telephone industry employees, volunteers their time and skills to developing equipment to meet very specific needs. They have developed a baseball game for blind persons; the ball and bases emit sounds. They have developed "talking" dolls for use primarily with emotionally disturbed children: a teacher can talk through the doll from another room. Also, they have developed numerous telephone variations utilizing lights, tactile readouts, and so forth for use by disabled individuals. The Pioneers can be contacted in many cities and towns across the country, where they are listed in the telephone book under "Telephone Pioneers of America."

To satisfy the equipment needs of all students, it may be necessary to purchase or borrow some highly specialized items. Students with limited use of arms or vision limitations require specialized equipment more often than other students do. Remember, however, that *not all* physically disabled and visually impaired students have unique equipment needs. When they do, many items can be obtained for them on loan from the National Library Service to the Blind and Physically Handicapped (Library of Congress) through regional depositories (often state libraries). Building-level, district-level, and regional-level special educators usually know what equipment particular students need; and they will help to locate and obtain the items.

In addition to the Library of Congress, equipment is available from organizations such as the American Foundation for the Blind which publishes a catalog (*Aids and Appliances*) of over 400 devices useful to visually impaired persons. Commercial companies also produce and sell specialized equipment for disabled students. Media specialists, nonetheless, can be aware of the kinds of equipment available and sources for obtaining them. Journals and commercial catalogs should be monitored for maintaining current awareness and so that information can be provided to special educators and others who are responsible for selection of specialized equipment. In addition, it may be the media specialist's responsibility to provide storage for, access to, and circulation of specialized equipment.

Only a small proportion of disabled students need highly specialized and expensive equipment; those who do are usually supplied with what they need through sources other than the media center. Where a piece of equipment means the difference between succeeding and failing in an educational setting, most likely the student will have access to that item. Where an item would make a positive difference in the quality and quantity of educational success for a student, but not the difference between success and failure, that item may be harder to supply. Media specialists can help in this regard.

The item may be too expensive for the school or school district to purchase for just one student. However, other funding sources are available. The school or student may apply for federal or state grant funds to purchase the item. Local service clubs, such as the Lions and Kiwanis organizations, are possibilities, as are local parent-teacher organizations and churches. Arrangements can vary:

- The item may be purchased for the student to keep.
- The item may be purchased and remain school property after the student leaves the school.
- The item may remain in the ownership of the funding source.
- The item may be rented or leased for the period of time the student is in the school.

See Chapters 10–16 on specific disabling conditions for suggestions on specialized equipment and related resources useful for individual types of disabilities.

SUMMARY

Meeting the equipment needs of disabled students in regular schools most often involves the effective utilization of standard media center equipment. Media specialists occasionally need to make simple modifications to regular equipment and only rarely need to purchase specialized equipment. The emphasis is on *effective innovative* usage of standard equipment rather than on *specialized* equipment.

In purchasing new equipment, media specialists should consider features that will encourage and facilitate usage by all students: simplified and well-placed controls, automatic features, durability, and versatility. Trends in equipment design and development are currently moving towards simplification (including new slot-loading projectors). Whenever possible, let the students "test" the piece of equipment prior to purchasing. Providing students with equipment that is easy to master will not only enhance the educational process, it will foster independence and free the media staff to work with more students personally.

REFERENCES

1. Inabeth Miller, "The Micros are Coming," *Media and Methods* 16 (8) (April, 1980): p. 33

2. Miller, p. 32.

3. Interview with Pat Konapatske, media specialist, Fern Ridge High School, Elmira, OR, January, 1980.

SELECTED RESOURCES—EQUIPMENT

Publications

EPIE Materials Report. Stony Brook, NY: EPIE Institute, Educational Products Information Exchange (EPIE). Bimonthly. Box 620, Stony Brook, NY 11790.

From October–June, the report includes the *EPIEGRAM* newsletter on equipment and material.

Organizations

American Foundation for the Blind, 15 W. 16th St., N.W., New York, NY 10011.

National Library Service to the Blind and Physically Handicapped, Library of Congress, 1291 Taylor St., N.W., Washington, DC 20542.

Chapter 9
Facilities and Environment

INTRODUCTION

This chapter will present ways to make the media center facility physically accessible to disabled students and its environment inviting and stimulating.

PHYSICAL BARRIERS

Section 504 of the Vocational Rehabilitation Act (PL 93-112) is the legislation which mandates "program accessibility" for all programs receiving federal aid:

- New facilities are required to be accessible and usable by disabled persons.
- One-of-a-kind programs conducted in existing facilities need to be accessible.
- Structural changes are required only if other means of providing access are not possible.

The law does not prescribe the means of making programs accessible. Where classroom instruction is concerned, it might be within the law to simply relocate the class to an accessible area. This is obviously not an option for the media center program. The media center itself and physical access (entry/exit) to that center are essential. Coupling Section 504 with PL 94-142's mandate for the "least restrictive environment" further magnifies the need to make it possible for all students to use the media center. The full media program must be accessible to each student, which may necessitate in some cases, structural and architectural modifications for the disabled student. The goal is to allow each student access with the greatest independence and the least loss of dignity.

Schools and school districts have, by now, developed plans for creating barrier-free environments in the schools in compliance with federal regulations. The media specialist does not have to know the specifications of these plans but should have a general awareness of whether they are being carried out. Make sure that the media center is barrier-free by consulting with the school principal. See the "Selected Resources" section at the end of this chapter for publications which can be referred to for detailed specifications.

It is not difficult to determine obvious barriers which actually prevent access to the center. But you will want to consult with the students themselves about more subtle restrictions and the ways those restrictions might be overcome.

Structural changes do not exclusively benefit the disabled. Consider, for example, the sloping curb corner on a sidewalk—it helps all types of people, including older people, or people pushing shopping carts or baby-strollers. Have you ever tried to get a cart of books or a project or piece of equipment up even a small flight of stairs?

Getting people into the media center is only the first step. Beyond the barriers of stairs, doors, doorsills, and turnstiles are the physical barriers of the center itself. The following points are important for the media specialist to consider:

- Traffic areas should be free of obstacles which restrict movement, such as trash containers, sculptures, furniture, plants, displays, or equipment.
- Obstacles such as door stops and raised outlets should be eliminated.
- Cords should never be left dangling from tables or equipment, or running across traffic areas.
- Doors should be all the way open or all the way shut.
- Drawers should be shut when not in use.
- Electrical outlets should be within short, safe reaching distance.
- Equipment should be stored for easy access, transport (carts for large or cumbersome pieces), and usage.
- Storage cupboards, drawers, and containers should open easily; open storage bins are preferable.
- Floors should not be slippery.
- Specialized furniture for the media center should be adapted for accessibility by students using special equipment such as wheelchairs or braces. For example:
  a. Circulation desks—a portion should be 33 inches high.

    b. Card catalog—low 16-inch base; drawers should go no higher than counter height; no pedestal bases.

    c. Shelving—at least 30 inches, preferably more, between stacks; no higher than 5 feet tall.

    d. Periodical holders—no higher than 5 feet tall.

All too often, schools have been designed to give teachers maximum control of students, to make cleaning and maintenance efficient, and to satisfy taxpayers. They have been designed for ''average'' students to receive a uniform education.

> It is interesting to note that school libraries and media centers have often been a step ahead of classrooms in their provisions for students as total persons with a variety of interests and needs. They were usually the first in schools to arrange facilities in a way that expresses the attitude that human beings are makers and users of knowledge, not just storers of it, and that mastery over materials comes with the freedom to discover new uses for them rather than fitting oneself to another's preconceived notions about use.[1]

It is the variety and diversity of the media center which makes it conducive to growth and learning. Media center personnel have been forerunners in realizing that different people learn best in varying situations. It should be a logical and simple step to sensitive accommodation of disabled people.

ENVIRONMENT

Even the removal of all physical barriers does not ensure an environment conducive to the needs of disabled students.

> An environment goes beyond facilities and actual physical space to those affective qualities of that space which influence persons within. It is composed of all the facilities and conditions in the surroundings and is experienced as ''felt space'' or ''what seems to be'' as well as ''what is'' . . . .[2]

The space in which we function affects the way we function or whether we function at all. The architecture or structure does contribute greatly to ''felt space.'' Having a variety of spaces is essential. Recognize the varying needs of students for quiet individual study areas, group work, equipment usage, production, group instruction, and audiovisual presentations. Some students function well with or even require strong stimulation (colors, sounds); others are distracted or overstimulated to the point of nonfunctioning. Furnishings must accommodate the student who works best reclining, as well as the student who works best at a desk or table. *Independence implies choices*. Creativity and imagination are seldom fostered by forcing conformity, by restricting the use of space and materials, or by being overly concerned about maintenance and order. Students must have options for meeting both their needs and their physical need to feel comfortable or ''at home'' in a situation.

> Every successful school media center is a place alive with activity and endeavors to make learning exciting. It is not a warehouse of materials, but it is a place emitting 'good vibrations,' as Harold Gores says. It is a place that accommodates a variety of activities for a diversity of people . . . It is a warm, human place, alive with ideas whose materials radiate the message 'use me'.[3]

''Good vibrations'' are created by many factors. Of primary importance is your attitude and friendliness as a media specialist, your willingness to relate to students as human beings, and your enthusiasm about what the center has to offer.

CONSIDERATIONS

Other elements to consider include:

Color. Studies have shown that color affects attitudes and that specific colors are conducive to specific activities. Provide areas which vary in color as they do in purpose, being aware of the lighting effects of that area, i.e., white in a large brightly lit area may be glaring and hard on the eyes, while it might pleasantly brighten a subdued corner. Finish and texture of colors/paint is also important in affecting glare or softness.

Plants. Plants help create a homelike atmosphere. They are a tie with the outdoors (where students would frequently rather be). They are alive and growing even when winter may make other vegetation dormant. Plant care can also be part of the educational process.

Noise. Be aware of distracting sounds and, as much as possible, schedule time and place of activities to minimize conflicting needs. Be aware that background music may drown out distracting noise for some, but actually be a distraction for others and also prevent some students from hearing what they need to hear. Poor acoustics create difficulty for hearing-impaired students, lessening, and even negating, intelligibility of sounds. Rectifying such a problem may involve installing sound screens and acoustical tiles. Noise is inherent with electric wheelchairs. Anticipate this and plan accordingly.

Lights. Lights are generally standardized, but extra lighting may be needed for some students; others may find regular light too glaring. Special shields and/or special lighting may be necessary to install in study carrels to meet the needs of students with particular vision problems. Remember that lighting goes far toward creating atmosphere and warmth.

Windows. Letting the outdoors in expands the environment. This can be particularly important for students who have less mobility. Windows are also the best source of lighting. Use shades to control glare, darken rooms, and, when necessary, remove distractions. Windows provide natural lighting for plants. Ideally windows should be low enough for students in wheelchairs to easily see out. The view from the window can be enhanced with creative landscape.

Displays. Design interest centers and displays to draw users to the media center, to stimulate discussion, to encourage project development and new interests, as well as to create a learning-centered atmosphere. Displays should include items that can be touched, examined, and manipulated.

Pets. Part of a learning and growing experience can be the care and observation of pets and animals. Specific responsibility should be assigned to students so the burden of care does not fall on the media specialist or on media center staff. Perhaps a pet in the media center could meet a nurturing need in some of the students.

Bulletin Boards. Board displays should be responsive to all students. Designate a specific space that students may use to publicize and disseminate information and as a forum for issues of concern. Other boards can be topical. Use large letter, 3-dimensional arrangements when possible; include textures, contrasting colors, symbols and illustrations, as well as words. Let students design and produce bulletin board displays. Include positive and equal representation of disabled persons.

Furnishings. Furnishings in the media center should possess the following qualities (most disabled students can use regular media center furniture):

Comfort as well as Function—What is comfortable for one student may be awkward for another. For example, a bean bag chair may be perfect for one student but impossible for another to even get in and out of; a padded chair may give one student needed support for working but be so relaxing as to put another to sleep. Some students work easily at tables; others need to spread out on the floor; others may require sloping surfaces or specially designed work trays. Being able to get close enough to a work surface is a comfort factor affecting those in wheelchairs. Carpeting can help create a homelike atmosphere, being especially comfortable for students who like to sit and work on the floor. It can absorb harsh sounds which may interfere with activities. However, it must be a short pile weave with tight loops in order to allow for easy wheelchair movement and traction for crutches. Long-pile shag carpets are like mud for students in wheelchairs and can trip students on crutches.

Sturdiness—Furniture must be sturdy enough to support an imbalance of weight so that a student will not topple over if s/he sits off-center on a chair or needs to lean for support on a chair, table, or bookcase. Fragile furniture is a barrier which inhibits most kids. It can be a strong source of embarrassment to a student who has difficulty with the fine motor movements, mobility, or bulky equipment such as braces. Both media staff and the students will be more comfortable if they don't have to worry about furniture breaking or collapsing. Items should be strong enough to withstand nonconventional usage and still retain their function and pleasant appearance.

Durability—Durability relates to using colors which will not show dirt, fabrics which will not show wear, paint which will adhere well to surfaces, plastics which will not crack, and wood which will not splinter and scratch.

Versatility—You should be able to move the furniture in the media center to accommodate changing needs. Tables should be designed so that they can be moved together or apart. They should be light enough so students can make the changes. Having some chairs and tables with adjustable height and angle control will help meet varying needs of students to get in close and at the right angle to their work. Apronless tables are needed by students in wheelchairs so that they can move in close. Even if all your tables are apronless, wheelchair-bound students still need a change in the furniture arrangement to provide more options. Items such as cubes and boxes can serve as chairs, footstools, tables, or storage, which will allow the students to decide the function of the item according to the need.

Areas. Create different environments by arranging furniture and decorations for specific activities. Some areas will need more stimulating colors, textures, posters, mobiles, etc. Others will need to be more subdued. Have areas where lighting can be adjusted, possibly shut off, for listening concentration. Arrange other spaces that will lend themselves to audiovisual presentations. Dimmer switches can be a useful way to control brightness of light for different purposes. Areas can be created in relationship to special features which already exist, such as a fireplace, a conversation pit, a reading tub, or a loft. Remember to adapt these special-feature areas for maximum accessibility: provide a ramp up to the loft area or down to the conversation pit, special handles or supports for getting into the reading/listening tub, etc.

Temperature. Be conscious of maintaining a constant temperature that is comfortable for students. Less active students may be cooler; think of their needs before opening windows. While a cooler room may keep some students awake, it could jeopardize the health of a student who is more susceptible to illness.

Labels and Signs. In order for disabled students to have the most independent use of the media center, shelves and storage must be clearly labeled using large tactile and/or 3-dimensional lettering, color codes, and symbols. In some cases, braille labels may be necessary. Directions and instructions for usage should be in a variety of formats. Provide large, clearly legible signs, which are easy to read and at varying heights; illustrations, diagrams, and maps of the center; and recorded information. Students should be made aware of all changes in location of media center materials and equipment; help, in the form of new guides, orientation, etc., may be necessary. Having a media center that is accessible to all students, in every sense of the word, is a concrete statement of your commitment to mainstreaming.

REFERENCES

1. Kay E. Vandergrift, "Person and Environment," *School Media Quarterly* 4 (4) (Summer 1976): 315.

2. Vandergrift, p. 311.

3. Paul W. Briggs, "School Media Center Architectural Requirements," *School Media Quarterly* 2 (3) (Spring 1974): 201.

SELECTED RESOURCES—FACILITIES AND ENVIRONMENT

Publications

Aiello, Barbara, ed. *Places and Spaces: Facilities Planning for Handicapped Children and Adults.* Reston, VA: Council for Exceptional Children, 1976.

> Designed to aid dialog between the educator and the designer (architect). Includes 3 sections: "In Print," (publications), "In Plan," (specifications) and "In Addition" (resources—people, groups, places).

Barrier-Free School Facilities for Handicapped Students. Arlington, VA: Educational Research Service, Inc., 1977.

> Summarizes suggestions, recommendations, and regulations that might be helpful to school officials in making educational facilities barrier-free for handicapped students.

Cary, Jane Randolph. *How to Create Interiors for the Disabled.* New York: Pantheon Books, 1978.

> A cheerful, optimistic, yet realistic picture of what is available today for adapting the home environment for someone who is disabled. Helps in

understanding some of the problems. Has ideas that could be used in the media center and would be a helpful resource for older students and parents.

Coons, Maggie, and Milner, Margaret, eds. *Creating an Accessible Campus*. Washington, DC: Association of Physical Plant Administrations of Universities and Colleges, 1978.

Besides giving specifications for creating a barrier-free campus, gives practical suggestions for implementation and also good background explanations of problems which are not readily apparent to someone who does not have to overcome them.

Hale, Glorya, ed. *Source Book for the Disabled*. New York: Paddington Press, Ltd, 1979.

An illustrated guide to easier and more independent living for physically disabled people, their families and friends. Provides helpful ideas for adapting media center environment.

Kliment, Stephen A. *Into the Mainstream: A Syllabus for a Barrier-Free Environment*. New York: American Institute of Architects, 1975.

Practical information for working toward a barrier-free environment in the community.

Organizations

American National Standards Institute (ANSI), 1430 Broadway, New York, NY 10018.

ANSI provides the machinery for creating voluntary architectural standards. State codes are often based on ANSI recommendations. They also publish a publication on funding sources for making changes.

PART III
Specific Disabling Conditions

Introduction to Part III

Chapters 10–16 provide suggestions for working with students who have specific disabilities. These are suggestions, not attempts to describe people with disabilities, nor prescriptions for ways to work with them. Under each heading, some examples of general characteristics have been provided to serve as guidelines. Some of these may apply to the specific individual's condition. For the best possible understanding you, as media specialist, must get to know the student personally and work with his/her special education and classroom teachers to determine specific needs. While the media specialist need not know in great depth either the cause of a disability or the medical specifications for that condition, it is necessary to know how a disability affects the student's ability to learn, to comprehend, and to communicate and what conditions in the media center will affect the student's health, safety, and comfort.

There is no such thing as a "typical" disabled person. In writing this book the attempt has been made not to place stigmatizing labels on people. Media specialists should be aware of the prejudices and injustices that are perpetuated when people are labeled, categorized, and stereotyped. People *have* disabilities; they are not the disability itself.

Most of the problems disabled people face come not from the disability, but from the reactions of other people toward them. They are treated differently and are often viewed with suspicion and discomfort because of fear and a lack of understanding on the part of others. Disabled students are children and adolescents—no better, no worse, than others. They should not be expected to act like adults: to be more patient, to be more understanding, or to be more stoic than other students their age. Nor should they be treated like babies: talked down to, restricted, denied the power to make decisions concerning their own lives, or not consulted on matters that affect them.

Perhaps there is a need to remind ourselves that the way people look or function physically is not indicative of their ability to think and feel. Blind people are often shouted at as if they were hearing-impaired, people with cerebral palsy are treated as if they cannot think, and retarded people are often treated like babies or animals who are unaware of people's rude remarks and behavior. Focusing on the person, not on the disability, can lead to rewarding relationships between the media specialist and the students and will afford students the opportunity to be themselves.

The following are suggestions for working with all disabled students:

- Make provisions and arrangements to include disabled students in all media center activities.
- Provide multisensory experiences with a wide variety of materials and formats.
- Encourage disabled students to take leadership roles.
- Apply the same rules to all students.
- Be a model to students and other teachers in relating to disabled students.
- Communicate and consult with special education and classroom teachers to maintain continuity with their programs of instruction and behavior management.
- Check with students to make sure they are comprehending; do not rely on appearances or expressions.
- Motivate but try not to frustrate.

SELECTED RESOURCES—SPECIFIC DISABLING CONDITIONS

Publications

Gearheart, William R., and Weishahn, Mel W. *The Handicapped Child in the Regular Classroom.* 2d ed. St. Louis, MO: Mosby, 1980.

> A very readable book, giving good basic coverage of the many aspects of education for disabled students. It speaks to specific disabling conditions and presents strategies, alternatives, modifications, and adaptations for educating these students.

Haring, Norris G., ed. *Behavior of Exceptional Children.* 2d ed. Columbus, OH: Charles E. Merrill, 1978.

> Defines "exceptional children," what their disabilities are, and the problems of labeling. Includes instruction for teaching exceptional children.

Journal of Special Education. New York: Grune and Stratton. Quarterly. Subscription Department, 111 Fifth Ave., New York, NY 10003.

> Provides background information and concrete suggestions which can be applied in day-to-day work with children.

Langone, John. *Goodbye Bedlam*. Waltham, MA: Little, Brown, 1974.

> A medical journalist explains in popular and concise terms how to understand abnormalities, character disorders, psychosomatic disorders, and brain dysfunctions. Useful for the nonspecialist who wishes to improve his/her understanding.

Reynolds, Maynard C., and Birch, Jack W. *Teaching Exceptional Children in All American Schools*. Reston, VA: Council for Exceptional Children, 1977.

> Clearly written text for all school personnel involved in interpreting and implementing PL 94-142. Half of book is devoted to specific handicapping conditions.

Organizations

American Association for the Education of the Severely/Profoundly Handicapped, 1600 W. Armory Way, Seattle, WA 98119.

American Library Association (ALA), Library Services to the Blind and Physically Handicapped, 50 E. Huron St., Chicago, IL 60611.

Clearinghouse on the Handicapped, 400 Maryland Ave., S.W., Washington, 20202.

Closer Look Information Center, 1201 16th St., N.W., Washington, DC 20036.

Developmental Disabilities Office, U. S. Department of Health and Human Services, 200 Independence Ave., S.W., Washington, DC 20201.

National Easter Seals Society for Crippled Children and Adults, 2023 W. Ogden Ave., Chicago, IL 60612.

National Foundation/March of Dimes, 1275 Mamaroneck Ave., White Plains, NY 10605.

Chapter 10
Learning-Disabled Students

CHARACTERISTICS

The general characteristics of the learning-disabled student are extremely varied.

> In testimony about Public Law 94-142, one congressman noted that there are 53 basic learning disabilities identified by research, that one person had identified 99 minimal brain dysfunctions, and that "no one really knows what a learning disability is."[1]

According to PL 94-142, a "specific learning disability" is defined as:

> . . . a disorder in one or more of the basic psychological processes involved in understanding or in using language, spoken or written, which may manifest itself in imperfect ability to listen, think, speak, read, write, spell, or to do mathematical calculations. The term includes such conditions as perceptual handicaps, brain injury, minimal brain dysfunction, dyslexia and developmental aphasia. The term does not include children who have learning problems which are primarily the result of visual, hearing, or motor handicaps, of mental retardations, or of environmental, cultural, or economic disadvantage.[2]

Learning-disabled students must be above the level of mental retardation and meet the criteria listed above, thus ruling out retardation as a factor in their learning problems. They must have a severe discrepancy between achievement and ability in one or more academic areas. Every student who does poorly in a subject does not have a learning disability. Learning disabilities are difficult to detect and diagnosis should be left to the experts, as with all disabilities.

However, if there is a student with an ascertained learning disability using the media center, as media specialist you will want to familiarize yourself with the specific characteristics and needs of that student. Consult with the student's special education teacher concerning (1) ways that you can come to a better understanding of the student's particular learning disability; (2) suggestions for materials you can consult specific to the individual problem; and (3) specific needs and suggestions for working with the student.

Remember that these students have the capacity to learn and can set and achieve goals as high as their peers.

The specific disorders of learning-disabled students often lead to them having problems with social interaction, exhibiting lack of organization, confusion, frustration, and difficulty following instructions and completing work. Such students become easily discouraged and often have low self-concepts.

Although the characteristics of learning-disabled students may be varied, the needs of these students are more uniform. They all have a need for quality individualized instruction. Through such instruction they can be taught to cope with their disabilities and to function effectively.

The following terminology may help in understanding the range of learning disabilities and conditions related to them:[3]

Agnosia. The inability to obtain information through one of the input channels or senses, despite the fact that the receiving organ itself is not impaired.

Aphasia. The impairment of the acquisition of symbols for a language system.

Cerebral Dominance. The control of activities by the brain, with one hemisphere usually considered consistently dominant over the other. In most individuals the left side of the brain controls language function, and is considered the dominant hemisphere.

Dyscalculia. The lack of ability to perform mathematical functions, usually associated with neurological dysfunction or brain damage.

Dyslexia. A disability in learning to read, resulting from neurological involvement.

Hyperactivity. An inordinate amount of motor activity or impulsiveness.

Hypoactivity. An inordinate lack of motor activity or impulsiveness.

Minimal Brain Dysfunction. A mild or minimal neurological abnormality which causes learning difficulties in the child with near average intelligence.

Neurophrenia. Behavior symptoms ensuing from central nervous system impairment.

Reversals. The child's inability to reproduce letters alone, letters in words, or words in sentences in their proper position in space or proper order.

Sound Blending. The ability to combine smoothly all the sounds or parts of a word into the whole.

Strephosymbolia. Perception of visual stimuli, especially words, in reversed or twisted order.

SERVICES FOR LEARNING-DISABLED STUDENTS

- Assist in developing and attend teacher inservice programs for understanding learning disabilities.
- Prepare handouts, diagrams, and charts for students to follow during presentations (to highlight important points, to illustrate, etc.)

INSTRUCTION

- Emphasize important points by such techniques as underlining, color highlighting, or repetition. Summarize at beginning and at end. Give students summaries, outlines, lists of main points, vocabulary sheets, etc.
- Make sure you get and keep students' attention while giving simple and systematic directions.
- Stand or sit close to student; arrange seating so there are few distractions between you and student.
- Use visuals for all presentations: transparencies, posters, diagrams, etc.
- Use a variety of formats for instructing, practice, review, and testing.

COLLECTION

In determining effective teaching materials, it is important to try materials on hand. If these are not as satisfactory as desired, check with the resource room teacher for supplementary materials which could be incorporated into the media center.

Books

- High interest/low vocabulary materials are appropriate; look for relevant illustrations.

Periodicals

- High interest/low vocabulary formats are useful; they provide a good source for visuals which support text.

Newspapers

- Newspapers should be tried with specific students to determine if typeface and style are effective.

Filmstrips

- Sound filmstrips are usually effective.
- Silent, captioned filmstrips need to be screened to determine level of vocabulary and whether information is conveyed by the picture alone if student cannot read the caption.
- Sound/captioned filmstrips are useful.

Films

- Interest levels of the student can be addressed even if student has difficulty reading.
- Effective since the content and concepts are presented visually.

Audiotapes and Discs

- These can be effective if used with visuals.

Slides and Transparencies

- They can be useful teaching media as they are usually accompanied by a discussion. Audio should be used to reinforce visuals.

Programed Materials

- Positive, immediate reinforcement is provided.

Graphics, Posters, Maps, and Globes

- These can be effective in small groups or if individual copies are provided for students to follow during presentations.

Games, Toys

- Students should be worked with to determine which items are most useful.
- Puppets and dolls are often effective with young children.

Models, Sculpture and Specimens

- These should be used with presentations allowing hands-on experience.

EQUIPMENT

There are several standard audiovisual equipment items that help media specialists provide for the individualized instruction of the learning-disabled students. Examples of these types of equipment include:

Magnetic Card Readers. Relatively inexpensive machines in which the student reads information on a card, records his/her response, listens to the correct answer recorded on the instructor track, and compares for accuracy and reinforcement. Prerecorded programs are available as well as blank cards. (One type is the Language Master.)

Electronic Keyboard Devices. Instruments allowing students to practice mathematical concepts and develop vocabulary skills. They are marketed under such brand names as Little Professor, Dataman, Spelling B, Speak and Spell, and First Watch.

Typewriters. Especially helpful for students with visual/motor problems which make writing difficult.

Calculators. A help to students who confuse numbers, columns, etc., in doing mathematical calculations.

Controlled Readers. Machines which can be set to regulate speed and which are useful for left to right progression of words, tracking, and teaching of speed reading.

Tape Recorders. Useful for taking notes; they also can be used as learning devices when used with headphones in study carrels (which reduce visual distractions). Student can use at own pace and replay material as needed.

Other Equipment. There are numerous electronic teaching machines available for purchase or lease which allow learning-disabled students to work individually on their reading, language and math skills. Check with a special education teacher in your school or district.

FACILITIES

- A study area should be provided, removed from the main flow of traffic. Limit auditory and visual stimulation in this area (e.g., posters, displays, or mobiles).
- A sufficient number of wired study carrels should be available.
- Signs and labels should be clear and concise; include picture symbols if possible. Too many signs are more confusing than helpful.
- Special centers, such as book nooks, should be developed.

REFERENCES

1. Phyllis Coyne, *Resource Booklet on Recreation and Leisure for the Developmentally Disabled* (Developed for Recreation and Leisure Skills Training Workshop at Portland State University), (April 1978): 4.

2. U.S. Department of Health, Education and Welfare, Office of Education, "Assistance to States for Education of Handicapped Children; Procedures for Evaluating Specific Learning Disabilities," *Federal Register* 42, no. 250, 29 December 1977, p. 65083.

3. Dave H. Martinez, "Learning Disabilities" (Unpublished dissertation, Portland State University, 1978) pp 4–5.

SELECTED RESOURCES—LEARNING-DISABLED STUDENTS

Publications

Henson, Ferris O., II. *Mainstreaming Children with Learning Disabilities.* Mainstreaming Series. Boston: Teaching Resources (formerly published by Austin, TX: Learning Concepts, 1977).

Journal of Learning Disabilities. Chicago, IL: Professional Press Inc. 10 issues per year. 101 E. Ontario St., Chicago, IL 60611.

McCartan, Kathleen W. *The Communicatively Disordered Child.* Mainstreaming Series. Boston: Teaching Resources (formerly published by Austin, TX: Learning Concepts, 1977).

Perceptions. Millburn, NJ: Perceptions, Inc. 8 issues per year. P.O. Box 142, Millburn, NJ 07041.
   The newsletter for parents of children with learning disabilities.

Stasios, Rosemarie, ed. *HELP for Emotional and Learning Problems.* Toronto, ON: Ontario Teachers' Federation, 1973.

Organizations

Association for Children with Learning Disabilities, 5225 Grace St., Pittsburgh, PA 15236.

Gesell Institute of Child Development, 310 Prospect St., New Haven, CT 06511.

Orton Society (for Dyslexia), 8415 Bellona Ln., Towson, MD 21204.

Chapter 11
Speech-Impaired Students

CHARACTERISTICS

A speech impairment is defined in PL 94-142 as " . . . a communication disorder, such as stuttering, impaired articulation, a language impairment, or voice impairment which adversely affects a child's educational performance."[1] The speech-impaired student's disability is generally limited to oral reproduction of speech and does not necessarily impede the learning process. This student is usually capable of using the existing audiovisual equipment and facilities of the media center without modification.

Even a minor speech or language problem, however, can affect a student's ability to communicate. It may also be a source of embarassment in relating to peers and thus limit a student's social and personal life and can cause emotional and behavioral problems. Students may also be reluctant to ask questions, ask for help, or participate in discussions.

Students with severe language/speech problems may not only have trouble expressing themselves, but may also have difficulty understanding others. Their preferred method of communication and understanding is usually visually oriented, using actions, gestures, and pictures. Some speech-impaired students are easily distracted visually and/or aurally, in which case, modifications made for learning-disabled students may also apply to speech-impaired. These would include having areas where auditory and visual stimulation are limited, and activity is at a minimum. Study carrels can be used to help facilitate concentration.

Severely speech-impaired students may drool, and it is customary for others to feel uncomfortable with this problem. Have paper towels readily available if there is a student with this condition.

Stuttering is a common speech impairment. The following are suggestions for working with students with this specific problem.[2]

1. Do not mention the stuttering; try to reduce the child's awareness of this problem.

2. Minimize those settings and situations that appear to cause increased stuttering.
3. Minimize conflict of all types when possible.
4. Encourage speaking when all is going well, and immediately minimize demands to communicate when stuttering becomes more pronounced.

STAFFING

- Be encouraging to speech-impaired students; give them opportunities for expressing themselves.
- Listen attentively and patiently and let these students finish their statements. (Do not fill in words and ends of sentences for them.)
- Provide a model for students by speaking in a normal tone and at a normal rate.

SERVICES

- Help design visuals to accompany audio presentations.
- Help record lessons on magnetic cards.
- Schedule times and places for students to work undisturbed and free from distractions.
- Schedule activities with small groups where students might be less inhibited about expressing themselves.
- Design activities where success is not dependent upon language/speech development (such as mime, nonsense jingles, songs, music, and art).

INSTRUCTION

- Provide opportunities for success in language production. Do not avoid language activities.
- Use open-ended questions requiring more than "yes" and "no" answers. Allow time for students to answer.
- Be conscious of possible distractions during instructional activities.
- Express ideas in a variety of ways.
- When students look bewildered or ask questions, rephrase statements.
- Let students use a puppet or "microphone" as a prop. Be aware of students' body language. Allowing students to use props and pick-

ing up on their body language may lessen inhibitions and provide students with security to express themselves.

- Introduce new concepts and new vocabulary prior to presentations.
- Work on building vocabulary, sequencing, and concept development.
- Use synonyms and a variety of descriptive words.

COLLECTION

- Use audiovisual combinations to reinforce language development.
- Provide materials for developing communication skills.

EQUIPMENT

- Use combinations of audio and visual, which are most effective.
- Furnish cassette recorders and headphones—useful for concentrated listening.
- Provide magnetic card readers.

FACILITIES

- Provide study areas removed from visual and auditory stimulation and activities.
- Work for an atmosphere that is relaxed.

REFERENCES

1. U.S. Department of Health, Education and Welfare, Office of Education, "Education of Handicapped Children; Implementation of Part B of the E.H.A.," *Federal Register* 42, no. 163, 23 August 1977, pp. 42478–79.

2. William R. Gearheart, and Mel Weishahn, *The Handicapped Child in the Regular Classroom* (St. Louis, MO: Mosby, 1976), p. 103.

SELECTED RESOURCES—SPEECH-IMPAIRED STUDENTS

Publications

Freeman, Gerald G. *Speech and Language Services and the Classroom Teacher*. Minneapolis, MN: National Support Systems Project, 1977.

McCartan, Kathleen W. *The Communicatively Disordered Child.* Mainstreaming Series. Boston: Teaching Resources (formerly published by Austin, TX: Learning Concepts, 1977).

Organizations

American Speech and Hearing Association, 10801 Rockville Pike, Rockville, MD 20852.

Trace Research and Development Center for the Severely Communicatively Handicapped, 1500 Highland Ave., Rm. 314, Madison, WI 53706.

Chapter 12
Orthopedically and Other
Health-Impaired Students

CHARACTERISTICS

"Orthopedically impaired" is described in PL 94-142 as:

> . . . a severe orthopedic impairment which adversely affects a child's educational performance. The term includes impairments caused by congenital anomaly (e.g., clubfoot, absence of some member, etc.), impairments caused by disease (e.g., poliomyelitis, bone tuberculosis, etc.), and impairments from other causes (e.g., cerebral palsy, amputations, and fractures or burns which cause contractures).
>
> 'Other health impaired' means limited strength, vitality or alertness, due to chronic or acute health problems such as a heart condition, tuberculosis, rheumatic fever, nephritis, asthma, sickle cell anemia, hemophilia, epilepsy, lead poisoning, leukemia, or diabetes, which adversely affects a child's educational performance.[1]

It is hoped that students with mobility problems will have the equipment they need to get around—wheelchairs, braces, crutches, walkers, canes, casts, etc. The media specialist's concern lies in making sure that the media center does not contain barriers (either physical or psychological) which will restrict the usage of such aids.

Beyond mobility restrictions, the media specialist must consider the student's ability to handle and manipulate materials and equipment. Particular emphasis on independent usage may necessitate modifications in storage accessibility and equipment adaptation. Special equipment will be needed only if the student has limited use of his/her arms. Consult with support personnel or physical therapists about meeting the unique needs of these students.

People in wheelchairs must perform pressure releases (i.e., shift positions, raise up, etc.), since sitting still for long periods is unhealthy. Also, constant intake of fluids is essential for kidney and bladder functioning; therefore, a "no drinking in media center" rule must be modified.

Physically disabled students may be educationally and socially delayed because of certain limitations of environmental and social experiences. Or, they may be more socially mature, having interacted primarily with adults who assist in daily care, transportation, etc. Their interests may reflect those of the adults they know, i.e., they may prefer reading, rather than socializing with their peers. And, because of limited involvement with peers, they may have difficulty with interpersonal relationships. They may have spent most of their lives in institutional settings or confined to their homes. Obesity may be a problem because of lack of exercise. Much of their learning may have been of one mode, such as reading, and may need to be balanced with hands-on experiential learning. Some students with severely limiting conditions have had to contend with rejection, prejudice, and personal injustice due to their physical appearances. Make involvement in the media center a positive, noncompetitive, success-oriented experience which meets the psychological, as well as physical, needs of all students.

STAFFING

- Familiarize yourself with procedures to follow when chronically ill students have seizures or attacks while under your supervision.
- Find out beforehand the best way to help a student in a wheelchair or braces who falls or becomes trapped by some obstruction.
- Find out if a student can or should be transferred from a wheelchair, and if so, what alternative seating (chairs, bean bags, pillows, etc.) is acceptable.
- Do not allow peers to push a student's wheelchair, unless special arrangements are made. Consult the special education teacher.

SERVICES

Processing

- Add heavy duty binding and reinforcement to materials for students with dexterity problems.
- Use lightweight binders for students with muscle weakness.
- Fasten clipboards to desk.
- Provide large pencils, pencil grips, or attach plastic golf balls or styrofoam balls on ends of pencils.

- Mount items, such as maps or pictures, for students who cannot work with these materials flat on a table or on the floor.
- Adapt packaging: add handles or tabs; reinforce; attach loops to items to be placed on higher shelves (use pole or barbeque tongs to get items down).
- Substitute or adapt game markers, making them more substantial and easier to grasp.

Special Events (Field Trips, Workshops, Fairs, etc.)

- Investigate and provide information about the destination and the accessibility of facilities.

INSTRUCTION

- Do not isolate less mobile students by conducting group activities in areas inaccessible to them (such as story wells, or raised platforms).
- Allow students sufficient time to select media and gather materials and supplies. Their independence is more important than a tight time schedule.
- If they cannot do it themselves, pair physically disabled students with students who can operate equipment and turn book pages, etc.
- Conduct activities with students sitting in chairs around wheelchair-bound students, so that peers are not always lower (sitting on floor) or higher (standing). Interact with students at eye level as often as possible.

EQUIPMENT

Easicorders. Tape recorders designed for note taking by the severely physically disabled.

Electric typewriters with keyboard shields. Especially helpful for the student with limited fine motor ability.

Automatic and "easy to operate" items. Auto-load 16mm film projectors, cassette recorders, as opposed to reel-to-reel tape recorders, and 8mm cartridge film loops are all useful.

Automatic page turners. Effective for students with severe arm and hand disabilities.

Adaptations. Controls should be changed so that they are operated with gross motor, rather than fine motor movements. Use large knobs, buttons, and levers. (See Chapter 8, ''Equipment.'') Bookrests should be available as well as push carts for crutch, walker, and cane users.

FACILITIES

Make sure that the media center is in compliance with federal regulations for a barrier-free environment by consulting with the school principal. In addition to the general specifications for the school, media center personnel should follow the guidelines below.

Shelving

- There should be at least 30 inches, preferably 30–36 inches, between stacks.
- T-base aisle shelving should be used, to allow wheelchairs to fit up to the shelves easily.
- Shelving should be no higher than 5 feet to allow chair-and-brace-bound students to reach media. Floor-level shelves may be inaccessible to students. (The average horizontal reach for chair users is 30 inches—with a range from 28 inches to 33 inches.)

Furniture

- All or most tables should accommodate wheelchairs, giving students choices of where to work.
- Primary tables should be 23 inches high, apronless, and without pedestal support base.
- Secondary tables should be 20 inches high, apronless, without pedestal support base, and with a 27-inch clearance underneath.
- Some table tops should be angled.
- If there are several wheelchair students in the school, fewer chairs are needed around tables, allowing for the extra space wheelchairs require.
- Chairs should be sturdy and well-balanced.
- Standing tables allow students in braces to stand with support; they should be placed throughout the center.
- Carrels should be 32 inches in width with a 27-inch clearance underneath to accommodate wheelchairs.
- Furniture should be arranged so that students have enough space to move around. Wheelchairs, crutches and braces require room to maneuver.

Card Catalogs

- There should be one section with a 16-inch base for easy access for a wheelchair or for students with braces or crutches.
- A pedestal base should be avoided.

Storage

Software:

- Open bins or shelves are preferable to cabinets and drawers. Low bases without crossbars are preferable.
- There should be an inconspicuous space for storage of adaptive equipment.

Hardware:

- Large items should be placed on low carts for easy lifting or for use from a chair.
- Small items should be on open shelves or tables.

Periodicals:

- Vertical holders should be a maximum of 5 feet high.
- Microfiche/film readers should be placed on tables of appropriate height.

Work areas:

- Low apronless counters are preferred.
- Sink should have no cabinet below, a drain at the back, and a winged faucet fixture up front.
- Pamphlets, pictures, clippings, etc., should be stored in lateral files.

Temperature

- Temperature should remain fairly constant and drafts or extreme changes in temperature should be avoided. Students in wheelchairs or who are physically disabled in other ways may not be able to move away from drafty areas easily. Chronically ill students may have low resistance to colds, etc.

Special Features

- If a turnstile is in the entranceway, an alternative entrance must be placed immediately beside it.
- Carpeting should be short pile weave with tight loops and nonskid materials to allow wheelchairs, braces, and crutches ease of move-

ment, while at the same time providing some friction to prevent slipping. Carpeting also cushions falls.

- Lever handles should be used when possible so that students with poor hand mobility or limited strength may open doors independently.
- Two-way doors should be lightweight with see-through sections.
- Furniture and shelving should be sturdy and well-balanced because lack of motor control may cause spilling or tipping.
- Display tables should have nonslip mats or covers.

COLLECTION

Books, Periodicals, and Newspapers

- Standard materials are usually appropriate.
- High interest/low vocabulary are appropriate for students who are educationally delayed due to difficulties in gaining normal living experiences.
- Tearproof books may complement the collection.
- Books may be rebound in spiral binders for ease in turning pages when lying flat.

Filmstrips, Films, Audiotapes and Discs, Slides, Transparencies

- These can be especially effective if students are educationally delayed, enabling them to enjoy high interest materials without the interference of reading difficulties.
- They provide vicarious experiences for students limited in mobility and experiences.

Graphics, Posters, Maps, Globes, Games, Toys, Models, Sculptures, and Specimens

- These items may be difficult to manipulate if they are oversized, flimsy, heavy, too small to grasp, or fragile.
- Many items can be modified to facilitate use; for instance (a) maps, posters, etc. can be laminated; (b) larger playing pieces can be substituted for small or flat pieces; and (c) trays should be provided to hold puzzle pieces.[2]
- Students should be paired when the size or nature of an item prevents comfortable or effective use by the physically disabled.

REFERENCES

1. U.S. Department of Health, Education and Welfare, Office of Education, "Education of Handicapped Children; Implementation of Part B of the E.H.A.," *Federal Register* 42, no. 163, 23 August 1977, p. 47478.

2. PEACHES (Pre-School Educational Adaptations for Children Who Are Handicapped), *For Your First Days with a Handicapped Child* (Portland, OR: Special Education Department, Portland State University, 1978), p. 3.

SELECTED RESOURCES—ORTHOPEDICALLY AND OTHER HEALTH-IMPAIRED STUDENTS

Publications

Fusco, Carol B. *Individually Prescribed Program of Instruction for Pupils Who Are Orthopedically Handicapped*. Columbia, SC: South Carolina State Department of Education, 1977 (This report is currently available through the ERIC system, number ED 140 558.)

Paraplegia News. Phoenix, AZ: Paralyzed Veterans of America. Monthly. 5201 N. 19th Ave., Suite 108, Phoenix, AZ 85015.

Programs for the Handicapped. Washington, DC: Office of Handicapped Individuals. Office for Human Development Services, Department of Education, 3130 Switzer Building, Washington, DC 20202.

Rehabilitation Literature. Chicago, IL: National Easter Seals Society for Crippled Children and Adults. Bimonthly. 2023 W. Ogden Ave., Chicago, IL 60612.

Organizations

American Cancer Society, 777 3rd Ave., New York, NY 10017.

Arthritis Foundation, 3400 Peachtree Rd., N.E., Suite 1101, Atlanta, GA 30326.

Cystic Fibrosis Foundation, 3379 Peachtree Rd., N.E., Atlanta, GA 30326.

Epilepsy Foundation of America, 1828 L St., N.W., Washington, D.C. 20036.

Leukemia Society of America, 211 E. 43rd St., New York, NY 10017.

Muscular Dystrophy Association, Inc., 810 7th Ave., New York, NY 10019.

National Association of the Physically Handicapped, 76 Elm St., London, OH 43140.

National Congress of Organizations of the Physically Handicapped, Inc., 7611 Oakland Ave., Minneapolis, MN 55423.

National Hemophilia Foundation, 25 W. 39th St., New York, NY 10018.

National Multiple Sclerosis Society, 205 E. 42nd St., New York, NY 10017.

United Cerebral Palsy Association, Inc., 66 E. 34th St., New York, NY 10016.

Chapter 13
Mentally Retarded Students

CHARACTERISTICS

PL 94-142 defines the ''mentally retarded'' condition as

> . . . significant subaverage general intellectual functioning existing concurrently with deficits in adaptive behavior and manifested during the developmental period, which adversely affects a child's educational performance.[1]

Historically, mentally retarded students enrolled in the public schools have been categorized into 2 main areas, depending on the severity of their mental retardation: the educable mentally retarded (EMR) and the trainable mentally retarded (TMR).

The current trend is to think in terms of degrees of mental retardation—mild, moderate, severe, or profound. By identifying where a student is on this continuous scale, individual learning needs in academic, social, and self-care skill areas can be assessed.

Some general but essential points to keep in mind when designing and implementing a program of media-related services for mentally retarded students are:

- Most retardation is mild for students enrolled in public schools.
- Most retarded students are educable.
- Curricular activities for mentally retarded students, as with all students, are on the same continua.

For the mild to moderately retarded student, learning occurs at a fairly even but less rapid rate than with most children. Academic and vocational needs parallel those of other students in the regular classroom. In working with students who are mentally retarded, the media specialist can view them as delayed in areas of development and behind their peers on an academic continuum, but not on a different track altogether. Apart from a slower rate of learning, most mentally retarded students should be able to use the media center without many modifications as it is designed for all students.

Students who are severely or profoundly mentally retarded will probably use the media center only under the direct supervision of the special education teacher. Frequent consultation and close cooperation between the media specialist and special education teachers are necessary in planning media center learning activities for these students.

STAFFING

- Reinforce good social behavior and appropriate participation.
- Model acceptable behavior.
- Use visual cues to reinforce verbal instructions.
- Routinize media center activities and procedures
- Know the student's abilities.

SERVICES

- Keep rules and procedures simple, clear, and consistent.
- Reinforce rules, procedures, and orientation information over a period of time.
- Help special education and classroom teachers produce single-concept learning materials.

INSTRUCTION

- Utilize a multisensory approach for teaching single concepts.
- Provide first-hand experiences as often as possible.
- Gear activities to students' abilities and interests.
- Use simple, consistent directions; increase number of directions gradually.
- Give students appropriate time to complete tasks.
- Model an action consistently, as when demonstrating equipment operation.
- Repeat instructions and lessons as applicable.
- Allow student to direct pace of instruction and practice activities.
- Break down tasks into discrete steps.
- Build on skills already mastered.

- Emphasize student's stronger learning modes but work to strengthen weaker modalities.
- Provide for a variety of responses based on individual skills and needs (e.g., allow the student to point, verbally identify, or signal).[2]

COLLECTION

Books. Emphasis should be placed on high interest/low vocabulary items. Primary and preschool levels are usually most appropriate for young children but students should not be limited to these. Higher level books may have illustrations which interest students (e.g., nature books with animal pictures). Some will read; others will enjoy being read to; others will enjoy the pictures.

Periodicals. These should have characteristics similar to books described above.

Newspapers. A variety of activities could be centered around the newspaper.

Filmstrips. Preschool and primary-level materials are effective for young children, especially those dealing with general life experiences. They are most effective with sound and in color. Older students will respond to subjects which interest them (use high interest/low vocabulary).

Films. These are similar to filmstrips in effectiveness, and much depends on the student's personal interest.

Audiotapes and Discs. They are especially effective in teaching music appreciation and story listening skills.

Slides and Transparencies. These media are effective for teaching signs and symbols, such as "exit," "danger," "poison"; or places in the community, etc.

Graphics, Posters, Maps and Globes. Their use depends on goals and level of materials used; single-concept, uncluttered, and colorful materials are most effective.

Models, Sculpture, Specimens. These are effective teaching media, but they are dependent on the level of the children and the goals of the lesson. Allow students to touch, hold, and manipulate.

EQUIPMENT

- Equipment usage should be based on individual ability and attention span. (Consider length of film, number of operation steps, etc.)

- Students should be encouraged to spend equal time with equipment designed for group usage and equipment designed for solitary usage.
- Rules for equipment operation should be brief and clear, and independent usage should be urged. Provide for repeated practice.
- As many automatic items as possible should be selected.
- Modifications and adaptations designed for use with students with other disabling conditions can be used with success by mentally retarded students, such as large print, and large functional control buttons and knobs.
- Students can learn to operate simple equipment or be paired with other students who can operate equipment.
- Audiovisual combinations are best.
- Cassette tapes and record players are effective for listening to music and recorded stories.

REFERENCES

1. U.S. Department of Health, Education and Welfare, Office of Education, "Education of Handicapped Children; Implementation of Part B of the E.H.A.," *Federal Register* 42, no. 163, 23 August 1977, p. 42478.

2. PEACHES (Pre-School Educational Adaptations for Children Who Are Handicapped), *For Your First Days with a Handicapped Child.* (Portland, OR: Special Education Department, Portland State University, 1978), p. 8.

SELECTED RESOURCES—MENTALLY RETARDED STUDENTS

Publications

Birch, Jack W. *Mainstreaming: Educable Mentally Retarded Children in Regular Classes.* Reston, VA: Council for Exceptional Children, 1974.

Fairchild, Thomas N., and Parks, A. Lee. *Mainstreaming the Mentally Retarded Child.* Mainstreaming Series. Boston: Teaching Resources (formerly published by Austin, TX: Learning Concepts, 1977).

Organizations

National Association for Retarded Citizens, 2709 Avenue E East, Arlington, TX 76011.

President's Committee on Mental Retardation, U.S. Department of Health and Human Services, ROB #3 Rm. 2614, 7th and D Sts., S.W., Washington, DC 20201.

Sex Information and Education Council of the U.S. (SIECUS), 137-155 N. Franklin St., Hempstead, NY 11550.

Chapter 14
Visually Impaired Students

CHARACTERISTICS

Visual impairments range from mild restrictions to total blindness. Special services, such as itinerant or resource teachers and specialized equipment, are available for students who are visually limited or blind.

PL 94-142 defines "visually handicapped" as:

> . . . visual impairment which even with correction adversely affects a child's educational performance. The term includes partially seeing and blind children.[1]

The following section from *When You Have a Visually Impaired Child in Your Classroom* expands on this definition:

> A child is generally considered eligible for the special services of a resource or itinerant teacher if his measured visual acuity is 20/70 or less in the better eye with corrective lenses; in other words, if what he can see at 20 feet is no more than what a person with normal vision sees at 70 feet. Children who have a measured visual acuity of 20/200 or less in the better corrected eye or who have a visual field of no greater than 20 degrees are classified as legally blind (a definition originally created to determine eligibility for public assistance). However, many of these youngsters are actually visual learners, some even functioning well with regular print.
>
> Children with field defects may have an inability to see peripherally or may have 'blind spots' in their visual fields.
>
> It is important, too, to be aware of the fact that visually disabled children differ in their ability to use their vision. Two children may have the same measured acuity, but one may rely on his other senses to perform the same tasks that the other child does by sight. The individual differences must be respected.
>
> Another consideration is the type of visual impairment, which is also a major factor in the child's visual functioning. With some eye disorders vision may actually fluctuate and even stable visual conditions may be temporarily influenced by factors such as lighting, fatigue, and emotions. The resource or itinerant teacher will discuss with you the specific needs or limitations related to your child's visual impairment.[2]

Educationally, the most important distinction to consider is whether a student, however he or she is classified, can be taught to read regular or large type print, or whether that student must be taught using means that do not involve sight. *Most can read print.*

It is easier to assess the educational needs of the student whose vision is severely limited, than it is to assess the needs of the student who is partially sighted. It is naturally correct to assume that the student with a severe visual impairment is receiving very little information visually about his/her environment. Therefore, information must be presented in auditory or tactile formats.

Assessing the educational needs of students whose vision is blurred or incomplete is difficult. It appears that the student understands the pictures in the workbook about which questions are being asked. It appears that the student is following the intricacies of play in a game. It appears that the student is able to travel safely at school and in the community. These students demonstrate the use of their vision regularly, but it is very difficult to determine how much or how well they are actually seeing. For example, a student describes a picture in a book: she sees a dog sitting and a girl standing. However, she does not see the dog begging or the cookie in the girl's outstretched hand. She misses the subtle information necessary for comprehending the picture. This is not an unusual situation; it demonstrates how vision classified as "functional" can be unreliable in learning situations.

STAFFING

- Beware of nonverbal communication.[3]
- Explain visuals as they are used.
- Allow students to sit where they can make the best use of whatever vision they have. Make sure that the location does not hamper their hearing or block the view of other students.
- Feel comfortable using words such as "see" and "look."
- Use verbal cues; state student's name to get his or her attention; state your name, if necessary, for recognition.
- Be sensitive to a student's unwillingness to use special appliances in front of peers. Take steps to lessen any stigma and to encourage use.
- Be consistent with other teachers (resource, itinerant, classroom) for methods in dealing with such behavior as head swaying and habitually looking down (common mannerisms for blind or severely visually impaired students).

- Encourage students to move about the media center to obtain materials and visual information. Students will know their own needs and develop ways of compensating for visual limitations.[4]
- Allow students to hold material close to their eyes.
- Plan for and encourage hands-on experiences.
- Be aware that a student's best vision may not be achieved by looking directly at a person or material; If peripheral vision is best, a turned face may not be a sign of inattention.[5]
- When guiding visually impaired students, allow them to hold onto your elbow (or wrist if they are shorter) and let them follow you.

SERVICES

- Label or code shelves, materials, equipment, and equipment controls with large type print, 3-dimensional or tactile letters, or braille, if necessary. (A braille label maker is available from the American Foundation for the Blind.)
- Develop a system for students to locate you or to get your attention if they are unable to see you. A bell? A light?
- Make a simple relief map of the media center. Use white glue which will dry to a hard finish or make perforated lines on the back with a sewing tracing wheel.
- Pair a sighted student with a visually impaired student when a new environment or experience could cause confusion or danger to the student.

PRODUCTION

- Outline copies of diagrams, maps, simple concept pictures, with white, hard drying glue or make perforated lines.
- Make duplications in black ink whenever possible. Photocopy or give originals to the visually impaired student rather than a ditto copy. The ditto master may also be given to the student; it is usually darker and more legible.[6]
- Use a large print typewriter.
- Produce single-concept slides, such as large letters of alphabet, or vocabulary words.

INSTRUCTION

- Whether or not the student uses vision or adapted materials, the visually impaired student will require longer work periods to complete assigned lessons. Allow time and a half, which is usually considered acceptable.[7]
- As students with vision problems may demonstrate eye fatigue, evaluate assignments beforehand to assess the amount of repetition required for mastery.
- Use concrete examples.
- Introduce one concept at a time.
- Do not stand with your back to a window. Glare and light will silhouette what you are doing.[8]
- Allow students to assist in demonstrations or to handle materials before or after demonstrations.[9]
- For a filmstrip with captions, have a sighted student read them aloud.
- Allow a sighted student with the same assignment to read the materials aloud to a visually impaired student.
- In test situations, permit students to write, type, dictate, or tape record their answers.
- If instructional materials need to be specially adapted (for example, brailled or tape recorded), give copies to the resource or itinerant teacher as far ahead of time as possible.[10]

COLLECTION

Books

- Regular print is usually appropriate as is, or appliances for magnification may be provided.
- Large print (synonymous with primary type) is most frequently used. However, beyond the third grade, not all curricula are available, due to high cost of production. Large print books are now available in standard sizes, rather than the oversized format used earlier, which makes them appear less obviously adapted and makes them easier to handle.
- Braille materials are available through the vision specialist serving the student.

- Reference books may present difficulties because of small type. They are often too large to store and too expensive to have brailled, printed in large type, or put on tape.
- Some metropolitan areas have volunteer services available for limited production or adaptation of materials.
- For legibility considerations, see Chapter 7, "The Media Collection."

Periodicals

- Regular print is usually appropriate as is, or appliances for magnification may be provided.
- Large print and brailled editions of many magazines are available through the Library of Congress and state libraries.

Newspapers

- Regular print is usually appropriate as is, or appliances for magnification may be provided.
- Local National Public Radio (NPR) radio stations are very effective sources for local and national news. Broadcasts may be taped for later use. (See end of Chapter 7, "Copyright Considerations.")

Sound films

- Sound filmstrips and films may be effective if essential information is conveyed via sound track. Thus, if students are not able to see all or any of the visuals, they will receive the information required to comprehend and to respond to questions.
- If necessary, additional information can be conveyed to visually impaired students if they are paired with sighted students who explain important visual activity on the film.
- A postfilm discussion will be helpful not only for visually impaired students, but for other students as well.

Silent Films

- Partially sighted students may be able to comprehend information presented if captions are read aloud and supplemented through discussion, but obviously silent movies are not effective except with students with milder visual impairments.
- Rear screen projections allow students to view more closely.

Audiotapes

- Tapes and discs are very effective learning media for the visually impaired student and are heavily relied upon throughout the student's education. However, listening in itself is often an incomplete experience.

Slides and Transparencies

- The standard method of projection on a large screen for group viewing is usually not effective. Rear screen projection is preferred. Often as the projection becomes smaller, it becomes clearer.
- Make prints from slides, or copies of the transparencies, for visually impaired students to use as the group watches the screen.

Graphics

- Single-concept, clearly outlined, or delineated areas are essential.
- Braille formats are occasionally available. However, research shows that these media are not effective learning aids for visually impaired students who likely have difficulty understanding the abstractions involved in map and globe reading.

Games

- Modifications for clarity may be helpful, such as dark outlines.
- Braille and large print editions are often available.

Models

- These need to be available for handling. The tactile sense is a valuable learning mode for items more intricate than the students' vision can ascertain.

Material[11]

- Felt tip pens: Black in varying widths should be used to produce bold letters or diagrams; use colors to highlight.
- Acetate: Usually preferred in yellow, when placed over the printed page it will tend to darken the print itself, as well as heighten the contrast from the background paper.
- Bold-line paper should be provided.
- Page markers and reading windows help students focus on words or lines of print.
- Sun visors and other shields are useful.
- Raised line paper should be available for some students.

- Templates and writing guides: These may be made out of cardboard, plastic, or metal. They are especially good for signing names.
- Bookstands bring work closer to students.

EQUIPMENT

Visually impaired students may need any of the following pieces of equipment to facilitate their educational programs. The equipment chosen for or by the student should allow for the greatest amount of independence and efficiency of use for that individual.

Talking Book Machines. Prerecorded record discs and audiotapes are available to anyone who is blind. The Library of Congress and state libraries are the major, but not sole, distributors of Talking Books and Talking Book Machines.

Variable Speed Tape. These machines enable users to review information at varying speeds, dependent upon individual needs.

Closed Circuit Television. This equipment will electronically enlarge printed materials onto a television screen. Contrast and brightness can be altered to improve viewing. Image can be reversed to white on black background.[12]

Optical to Tactile Converter. A device about the size of a portable cassette tape recorder, it converts print into tactile letters when a small probe is passed over a line of print.

Slide Projectors. Teacher-produced slides can aid reading for visually impaired students by allowing them to view the alphabet and basic reading vocabulary in a size and brightness that most adequately meets their own unique visual needs.

Magnifiers. There are several types of magnification instruments that can aid visually impaired students in reading print materials. One of the most efficient is one which maintains a constant distance from the printed materials and requires that the student only move the device left to right.

Microfiche Enlarger. A special lens will enlarge the visual image on the screen of a microfiche reader. However, poor contrast or insufficient lighting may still present problems.

Brailler. This device can help blind students record information for their own or other blind students' use.

Braille Slate and Stylus. This combination can be used to take notes in braille.

Rear Screen Projectors. They allow students to get very close to the screen.

Portable Cassette Recorders. A large range of uses for visually impaired students are provided—note taking, recording for transcription, etc.

Speech Compressors. These devices speed up recorded material without changing the pitch.

Telescopic Aids. Small telescopes are available for viewing at a distance.

Lamps with Rheostates. These provide for variations (higher or lower intensities) in lighting.[13]

Other Sophisticated Hardware. The Kurzweil Reading Machine, for example, is available for use with visually disabled students. However, currently the cost is prohibitive for most public schools. They are most often used in special schools with high populations of blind students.

FACILITIES

- Leave doors and cupboards either all the way open or all the way closed.
- Lighting: Provide different areas that are highly illuminated and dimly lit; students with visual impairments vary in their lighting preferences.
- Provide necessary work or storage space to accommodate special materials and/or equipment.[14]
- Have an uncluttered floor plan.
- Alert students to any relocation of furnishings.

Bulletin Boards[15]

- Use sharp contrasting colors.
- Use 3-dimensional objects when possible.
- Avoid straight pins and other protruding objects within students' height range. Staples and thumbtacks are less dangerous.
- Arrange some bulletin board displays to be examined by touching. Always remember the disadvantage for a visually impaired student in any situation in which a model or a picture is used as an abstract of the real object.
- Place hanging mobiles—which would otherwise come near the floor—over the center of a table.

- Orient students to any object which is sharp or fragile; demonstrate its position and placement.
- Arrange displays on tables so that low items are in front and high ones are in back.
- Arrange items in categories.
- Keep similar objects separated so they can be distinguished.
- Describe items which cannot be distinguished without vision.
- Provide tape recorded tours using tactile clues to locate objects on any display tables.

REFERENCES

1. U.S. Department of Health, Education and Welfare, Office of Education, "Education of Handicapped Children, Implementation of Part B of the E.H.A.," *Federal Register* 42, no. 163, 23 August 1977, p. 42479.

2. Anne Lesley Corn and Iris Martinez, *When You Have a Visually Impaired Child in Your Classroom: Suggestions for Teachers* (New York: American Foundation for the Blind, 1977), p. 4.

3. Ardis Ruark and Carole Melby, *Kangaroo Kapers or How to Jump into Library Services for the Handicapped,* (Pierre, SD: Division of Elementary and Secondary Education, 1978), p. 8.

4. Corn and Martinez, p. 5.

5. PEACHES (Pre-School Educational Adaptations for Children Who Are Handicapped), *For Your First Days with a Handicapped Child* (Portland, OR: Special Education Department, Portland State University, 1978), p. 1.

6. Corn and Martinez, p. 15.

7. Corn and Martinez, p. 15.

8. Corn and Martinez, p. 13.

9. Corn and Martinez, p. 13.

10. Corn and Martinez, p. 14.

11. Corn and Martinez, pp. 8–10.

12. Corn and Martinez, p. 11.

13. Corn and Martinez, p. 9.

14. Corn and Martinez, p. 9.

15. PEACHES, p. 7.

SELECTED RESOURCES—VISUALLY IMPAIRED STUDENTS

Publications

Corn, Anne Lesley, and Martinez, Iris. *When You Have a Visually Impaired Child in Your Classroom: Suggestions for Teachers*. New York: American Foundation for the Blind, 1977.

Large Type Books in Print. New York: R. R. Bowker Co., 1980.

Martin, Glenda J., and Hoben, Millie. *Supporting Visually Impaired Students in the Mainstream*. Reston, VA: Council for Exceptional Children, 1977.

Orlansky, Michael D. *Mainstreaming the Visually Impaired Child*. Mainstreaming Series. Boston: Teaching Resources (formerly published by Austin, TX: Learning Concepts, 1977).

Organizations

American Foundation for the Blind, 15 W. 16 St., New York, NY 10011.

American Library Association, Library Services to the Blind and Physically Handicapped, 50 E. Huron St., Chicago, IL 60611.

American Printing House for the Blind, 1839 Frankfort Ave., Louisville, KY 40206.

Association for Education of the Visually Handicapped, 919 Walnut St., Fourth Floor, Philadelphia, PA 19107.

National Library Service for the Blind and Physically Handicapped, Library of Congress, 1291 Taylor St., N.W., Washington, DC 20542.

Recording for the Blind, 215 E. 58th St., New York, NY 10022.

Chapter 15
Deaf and Hard-of-Hearing Students

CHARACTERISTICS

This section combines deaf and hard-of-hearing categories. They are defined in PL 94-142 as follows:

> 'Deaf' means a hearing impairment that is so severe that the child is impaired in processing linguistic information through hearing, with or without amplification, which adversely affects education performance. 'Hard of hearing' means a hearing impairment, whether permanent or fluctuating, which adversely affects a child's educational performance but which is not included under the definition of 'deaf.'[1]

Students with hearing impairments vary considerably in degrees of hearing loss and in their ability to use whatever hearing they might have (residual hearing). Hard-of-hearing students are characterized by mild to moderate articulation problems and language delay. Students who are labeled deaf are characterized by severe articulation problems and language delay and may be unable to understand spoken or written language and/or to express themselves at the level of their peers.

Being deaf is much more than simply not being able to hear. Mastering speech and developing (even being aware of) the language patterns that underlie written and oral communication are formidable tasks for the hearing-impaired. Most of what deaf children learn is taught to them. They absorb or "catch on" to less information by themselves; they experience a " . . . lack of incidental 'overhead' learning."[2] It may be difficult for hearing-impaired students to deal with abstractions and to make logical transferences of information from one situation to another. They are often isolated from their families, peers, and their environment as a result of their lack of communication skills and lack of understanding.

Hearing-impaired persons use different methods of communication. Many, even those defined as legally deaf, have some "residual hearing." They may hear sounds within certain ranges or be able to detect variations that serve as cues. Hearing aids amplify only those sounds within that range and do not provide full hearing capacity. Use of residual hearing may be augmented with lip reading. By learning to carefully watch and listen, some hearing-impaired people can learn to speak. This "oral" method requires long years of training; it is often not possible for some hearing-impaired persons to develop these skills. When individuals can learn "oral" communication, they can usually function quite normally in general society.

Another method of communicating is sign language. Signing can be taught to hearing-impaired children at a very young age and they can more quickly learn to communicate than if they have to rely totally on oral communication. Finger spelling is one aspect of signing in which the letters are individually formed, rather than forming a sign for an entire word or thought, which is another type of signing. The disadvantage of signing is that communication in this form is limited to only those who know sign language.

Total communication is the term used to describe the combination of oral communication and signing. Proponents claim that it is logical to make use of all forms of communication within an individual's ability. Critics, however, feel that total communication ends up primarily as a signing activity because it is easier for an individual with a severe hearing impairment to learn and to use signs.

There is a great deal of controversy over which method of communication is best. Which approach an individual student will use in communicating is a decision made by the parents and possibly by the student. The media specialist should respect and abide by their decision. Do not try to change or supplement their preferred method.

Sign language, finger spelling, speaking and writing are all dependent upon mastery of basic langauage skills. As a media specialist, you should encourage the development of these skills. Encourage students to communicate through their chosen mode and to actively participate with their peers in activities and discussions. (Discourage them from always writing.) Communication and interaction with others and the environment decreases the sense of isolation hearing-impaired students may feel. This type of climate is necessary for learning to take place.

STAFFING

- Ask open-ended questions to determine a hearing-impaired student's level of understanding.
- Speak on a face-to-face level and maintain eye contact.
- Articulate clearly with moderate speed. Avoid exaggeration, mumbling, or loud speech.

- Speak to the side of the better ear if you are aware of a need to do this.
- Learn a few of the basic signs, if sign language is the major mode of communication for a student.
- Hearing aids pick up and amplify ambient (background) noise; with this in mind, conduct conversations in quiet areas.
- Make sure that the student is aware that you are about to give a direction, etc. It is helpful if the student can anticipate the nature of any communication.
- Encourage students to ask you to repeat and rephrase statements they do not understand.
- Face the light when you are talking.

SERVICES

- Because language difficulties can result in reluctant readers, create incentive programs which will encourage reading.
- Develop programs that use and encourage expressional activities such as puppetry, drama, or mime.

Procedures

- Write captions under media on transparencies, slides, filmstrips, or videotapes.
- Write captions on separate films/slides and project side by side simultaneously using 2 projectors.
- Mount slides together (picture on one, caption on another).
- Before captioning video productions, consider the following. There should be:
  a. Minimum background noise or music in the media.
  b. No off-camera narrator while the talking face of another person is shown.
  c. No fast dialogs.
  d. A minimum of transition between off- and on-camera speaker.
  e. Moderate-paced narration.
- Create single concept materials from slides, filmstrips, 8mm film loops, transparencies, etc.
- Reproduce maps that feature single concepts (such as only physical features or a state outline).[3]

INSTRUCTION

- Seat hearing-impaired students for a good view of the instructor, the activity, and other students. Point to the person who is speaking to help the hearing-impaired student easily locate the speaker.
- Do not stand in front of windows or bright lights when addressing hearing-impaired students.
- Before discussing new material, list key vocabulary on handouts, board, overhead, etc.
- Use visual cues—captioned films, puppets, filmstrips, flannel boards, pictures. Use props to introduce vocabulary; use words that can be acted out.
- Present information, stories, and so forth, in a logical sequence.
- Be concise, precise, but comprehensive in your directions.
- Relax, smile, speak clearly and distinctly, but do not exaggerate or speak too loudly.
- Demonstrate whenever possible.
- Provide multisensory experiences.
- Use hands-on experiences.
- If necessary, interpret what student says to group.
- Have written scripts for students to read while they are looking at visuals.

COLLECTION

- Media considerations for the hearing-impaired and deaf: Materials should be action-filled and very organized, with logical concept development definitions.
- The majority of content and concepts should be shown rather than spoken.
- Audiovisual media should be paced slowly enough to allow time for students to read caption and see visual.
- Simple vocabulary and language structures are most appropriate. (There should be a minimum of idioms, passive sentences, negatives, and complex sentences.)[4]

Books

- Regular collection is generally appropriate.
- High interest/low vocabulary items will be effective for those whose reading skills lag behind their interest.

- Most curriculum programs for the deaf use a sight vocabulary approach, rather than a phonic or linguistic-based type.
- Reference Books: Because of limited reading skills, hearing-impaired students may have difficulty using reference tools.

Periodicals

- Magazines which combine visuals with words reinforce language development. Consider vocabulary limitations of hearing-impaired students: They don't "pick up" words.

Newspapers

- There is no special need for adaptation.
- Newspapers published around the country by state schools for the deaf are available.
- Periodicals and newspapers may have lower reading levels, but they also use many idioms, coined words and colloquialisms that may present difficulties for some students.

Filmstrips

- Sound filmstrips may be effective if the student has some residual hearing or if the print and visual information provides adequate information.
- Captioned filmstrips are usually very effective. The vocabulary should be within the student's skill level or new vocabulary should be introduced prior to viewing. The student can use filmstrips independently at his/her own speed.

Films

- 16mm movies should be previewed with the sound off, which will determine whether the information provided through the visual portion of a film is adequate to convey the information in the lesson to hearing-impaired students.
- Captioned films for the deaf are appropriate for use. These can be acquired through the state school for the deaf, the state bureau of education for the handicapped, or further information can be obtained from the state division of vocational rehabilitation, the state department for the deaf and Gallaudet College. (See "Selected Resources" section at the end of this chapter.)
- Videotape can be captioned; avoid long dialogs.
- Since they rely on visuals for providing essential information, 8mm movies and film loops are effective.

Audiotapes and Discs

- These are not appropriate for learning unless sufficient amplification through the headphones is possible.

Slides

- Because they rely on the use of vision, they are effective teaching media.

Graphics, Posters, Maps and Globes

- They are effective media for teaching hearing-impaired students.

Games and Toys

- If they rely on vision, they are useful teaching media. If games are based on sounds, as some phonic drill games are, alternatives should be offered.

Models, Sculptures, and Specimens

- They allow hands-on experience and are effective.

Transparencies

- They are easily made, stored, and viewed by a group.
- They promote the teaching of single concepts.

EQUIPMENT

Amplification Equipment

- Headphones/earphones—A specialist should be consulted before using. With earphones, hearing aids must be removed and consequently there is no way of monitoring the exact sound level. It is best to leave hearing aids on and use record players, etc., in the same fashion as with hearing students.[5]
- Audio loops and wireless headphones—Some will amplify through a student's hearing aid. (Check with a specialist.)

Slide/Filmstrip Projectors and 8mm Loop Projectors

- Students can use independently at their own speed or repeat as needed.

Overhead Projectors

- They allow presenter to face audience.

- The projection light enhances the face of the speaker and makes lip reading easier.

16mm Projectors

- They can be used for showing captioned films.

Character Generators

- They can be used to caption video productions.

FACILITIES

- Quiet listening and study areas, free from distractions, should be provided.
- Visual signals should be installed to augment bells and fire alarms.

REFERENCES

1. U.S. Department of Health, Education and Welfare, Office of Education, "Education of Handicapped Children, Implementation of Part B of the E.H.A.," *Federal Register* 42, no. 163, 23 August 1977, p. 42478.

2. Linda Bardenstein, *Selection and Adaptation of Media for the Deaf* (Rochester, NY: National Technical Institute for the Deaf, no date), p. 1.

3. Bardenstein, p. 1.

4. Bardenstein, p. 1.

5. PEACHES (Pre-School Educational Adaptations for Children Who Are Handicapped), *For Your First Days with a Handicapped Child* (Portland, OR: Special Education Department, Portland State University, 1978), p. 15.

SELECTED RESOURCES—DEAF AND HARD-OF-HEARING STUDENTS

Publications

Birch, Jack W. *Hearing Impaired Pupils in the Mainstream*. Reston, VA: Council for Exceptional Children, 1976.

Davis, Julia, ed. *Our Forgotten Children: Hard-of-Hearing Pupils in the Regular Classroom*. Minneapolis, MN: National Support Systems Project, 1977.

Mainstreaming the Hearing Impaired Child: An Educational Alternative. Mainstreaming Series. Boston: Teaching Resources (formerly published by Austin, TX: Learning Concepts, 1977).

McCarr, Dorothy, and Wisser, Mary W., compilers. *Curriculum Materials Useful for the Hearing Impaired.* Beaverton, OR: Dormac, 1979.

Organizations

Academy of Rehabilitative Audiology, Speech and Hearing Science Section, Department of Communications, 325 Derby Hall, Ohio State University, Columbus, OH 43210.

Alexander Graham Bell Association for the Deaf (for Information on Aural/Oral Communication), 3417 Volta Pl., N.W., Washington, DC 20007.

Bureau of Education for the Handicapped, Captioned Films and Telecommunications Branch, U.S. Office of Education, Washington, DC 20202.

Captioned Films for the Deaf Distribution Center, 5034 Wisconsin Ave., N.W., Washington, DC 20016.

Closed-Captioned Television, 1443 Beachwood Dr., Hollywood, CA 90028.

Gallaudet College and Press (for Information on ''Total'' Communication), Kendall Green, N.E., Washington, DC 20002.

National Association of the Deaf, 814 Thayer Ave., Silver Springs, MD 20910.

Chapter 16
Seriously Emotionally Disturbed Students

CHARACTERISTICS

PL 94-142 defines "seriously emotionally disturbed" as follows:

> The term means a condition exhibiting one or more of the following characteristics over a long period of time and to a marked degree, which adversely affects educational performance;
> An inability to learn which cannot be explained by intellectual, sensory, or health factors;
> An inability to build or maintain satisfactory interpersonal relationships with peers and teachers;
> Inappropriate types of behavior or feelings under normal circumstances;
> A general pervasive mood of unhappiness or depression; or
> A tendency to develop physical symptoms or fears associated with personal or school problems.
> The term includes children who are schizophrenic or autistic. The term does not include children who are socially maladjusted, unless it is determined that they are seriously emotionally disturbed.[1]

Seriously emotionally disturbed students may have difficulty learning because their behavior can interrupt the learning process. Working with emotionally disabled students should involve a thoughtfully planned and consistent approach by all teachers concerned. Emphasis should be on structured activities for success and on developing strong interpersonal relationships with the student.

Remember that students who demonstrate unacceptable behaviors are not necessarily seriously emotionally disturbed.

> Since there are few, if any, behaviors that are exclusive to "emotionally disturbed children" which are not found in so-called "normal children," it follows that children who exhibit inappropriate behaviors are individually "mostly just kids." Treat them as individual children.[2]

The emotionally handicapped student may or may not express any of the typical behavior disorders while in the media center, depending upon his/her personal associations with it. The environment created by the media specialist is an important factor in making the student feel comfortable and will encourage a "normal" attitude toward the facility and the media program.

Other factors besides the environment, however, influence behavior. Do not be discouraged if, in spite of your efforts, the student expresses inappropriate behavior. Consult with the special education and classroom teacher to coordinate programs of discipline, expectations, and reinforcements for appropriate behavior.

Do not allow destruction and/or abuse of people or things. For the individual, a sense of security can result from having limits defined and guides for appropriate behavior set forth.

STAFFING

- Make an extra effort to commend appropriate behaviors of both the student and his/her peers.[3]
- Provide a consistent reaction to inappropriate behavior which is nonreinforcing to the student (ignoring, removal, or loss of privilege, etc.).[4]
- Recognize students' feelings and respond with flexibility and sensitivity, not oversensitivity.[5]
- Stress your role of "manager" in encouraging the student's independence and initiative and channeling the student's energies constructively.[6]
- Never cause a student to feel "concerned"; provide acceptable options for behavior.[7]
- Model appropriate behavior; be calm and controlled; do not shout.

SERVICES

- Keep rules and procedures simple and clear.
- Establish specific rules for behavior (not just "Be good!").

INSTRUCTION

- Keep directions brief and clear.
- Have student repeat or write down directions.

- Require frequent student response or interaction.[8]
- Structure activities around student's interests.
- Keep activities short in length; limit waiting time or unstructured time between activities.[9]
- Pace activities; try to provide active, followed by quiet, activity.[10]
- Pair students with positive behavior models.
- Position student next to or near you.
- Plan activities within the ability range of student to avoid frustration; watch for low frustration tolerance.
- Ask open-ended questions and encourage verbal responses from withdrawn students.

COLLECTION

Books, Periodicals, and Newspapers

- The standard collection is appropriate.
- High interest/low vocabulary items are helpful for students who are educationally delayed.

Filmstrip and Films

- Sound filmstrips, 16mm films, and 8mm filmloops are especially effective as they enable students to manage material of interest without the problems associated with reading and vocabulary delay.
- Captioned filmstrips need to be assessed for the ability of their visual cues to convey information, especially where vocabulary is difficult.

Audiotapes and Discs

- These are very effective teaching/learning media, especially where headphones are utilized to encourage concentration and to limit distractions.

Slides, Transparencies, Graphics, Posters, Maps, Globes, Games, Toys, Models, Sculpture, and Specimens

- No unique adaptations or considerations are identified.

EQUIPMENT

- Equipment usage should be supervised and attention paid to operation safety.

- Installation and use of audio loops with wireless headphones allow students to feel less confined.
- Avoid excessive use of equipment with withdrawn students if it further isolates them from personal interaction.[11]

FACILITIES

- Create a quiet, relaxed atmosphere (highly stimulating situations can precipitate a loss of control).
- Provide soft, comfortable furniture.
- Provide study areas away from the main flow of traffic and away from other distractions such as doors, windows, or equipment.
- Make wired study carrels available in sufficient numbers.
- Eliminate visual distractions in study areas, e.g., posters, graphics, mobiles, displays, or bulletin boards.
- Provide enough space for each student.
  Research has shown that he (the emotionally impaired student) tends to require more physical space than his peers so the same square footage can accommodate fewer students. Crowding leads to a build-up of tensions and consequently a reduced ability to function.[12]
- Provide a "cool-off" space.

REFERENCES

1. U.S. Department of Health, Education and Welfare, Office of Education, "Education of Handicapped Children, Implementation of Part B of the E.H.A.," *Federal Register* 42, no. 163, 23 August 1977, p. 42478.

2. PEACHES (Pre-School Educational Adaptations for Children Who Are Handicapped), *For Your First Days with a Handicapped Child* (Portland, OR: Special Education Department, Portland State University, 1978), p. 1.

3. PEACHES, p. 2.

4. PEACHES, p. 2.

5. Pamela Bodoin Smith and Glee Ingram Bentley, *Participant Manual, Mainstreaming. (Teacher Training Program): Mainstreaming Mildly Handicapped Students into the Regular Classroom* (Austin, TX: Education Service Center, Region XIII, 1975), p. 32.

6. Smith and Bentley, p. 32.

7. Smith and Bentley, p. 32.

8. PEACHES, p. 12.

9. PEACHES, p. 9.

10. PEACHES, p. 14.

11. PEACHES, p. 15.

12. Karen Harris and Barbara Baskin, *The Exceptional Child in the School Library: Identification and Accommodation* (Washington, DC: U.S. Educational Resources Information Center, ERIC Document ED 097 897), p. 9.

SELECTED RESOURCES—SERIOUSLY EMOTIONALLY DISTURBED STUDENTS

Publications

Deno, E. N. *Educating Children with Emotional, Learning and Behavior Problems.* Minneapolis, MN: National Support Systems Project, 1979.

Parks, A. Lee. *Behavior Disorders: Helping Children with Behaviorial Problems.* Mainstreaming Series. Boston: Teaching Resources (formerly published at Austin, TX: Learning Concepts, 1976).

Stasios, Rosemarie, ed. *HELP for Emotional and Learning Problems.* Toronto, ON: Ontario Teachers' Federation, 1973.

Organizations

Mental Health Materials Center, 419 Park Ave., S., New York, NY 10016.

National Society for Autistic Children, 306 31st St., Huntington, WV 25702.

PART IV
Assessment and Planning

Chapter 17
Assessment Guide and Related Materials

Chapter 17 provides an assessment tool and related materials for use in assessing the media center program in terms of how currently effective it is in meeting the needs of mainstreamed disabled students. After completing the assessment, Parts I, II, and III of this book can be referred to for practical strategies and suggestions, both general and specific, for developing and implementing a plan of action to modify the existing program, according to particular types of disabled students in the school. The profile graphs at the end of this chapter and the plan of action forms and procedures in Chapter 18 will facilitate planning.

INSTRUCTIONS FOR COMPLETING THE ASSESSMENT GUIDE AND SCORING PROCEDURES

Work on this "Assessment Guide" activity in more than one sitting. Select a quiet place where you can work uninterrupted for 30–45-minute periods. Base your responses on your *initial*, immediate reaction to each statement.

Letters refer to example in Figure 1.

A The "Assessment Guide" consists of 38 goal statements.

B Each goal statement is followed by a set of indicators lettered *a*, *b*, *c*, etc. These indicators are tasks which might be performed to achieve the specific goals.

C Using the scale, determine whether you are actually performing the task and at what level. (See the more detailed explanation, "Rating Scale Key," on page 152.) Do not be concerned at this point about the reasons for performing or not performing a task or even an entire set of tasks. These reasons will be considered when you develop your plan of action, (discussed in Chapter 18). For instance, in Figure 1, indicator items *c, e, f* are rated "0" because the media specialist does not do them. Even though item *e* is performed by the special education teacher and item *f* by the classroom teacher, they are still rated "0."

D Each indicator is to be rated in terms of *your individual performance* (as media specialist) by circling the appropriate response to the right of each item: 0 1 2 3 4 5

Figure 1

9. Goal Statement

A { **The media specialist helps nondisabled students to communicate and relate positively to disabled students.**

The media specialist: **D**

a. Provides informational materials about dis-   0 1 2 3 4 5
abling conditions.

b. Makes media available (fiction, nonfiction,   0 1 2 3 4 5
print, nonprint) which present a positive,
fair, and balanced representation of disabled persons.

c. Addresses attitudinal changes through liter-   0 1 2 3 4 5
ature, films, speakers, and experiential
activities.

B {

d. Utilizes materials that accustom students to   0 1 2 3 4 5
seeing, hearing, and reading about disabled
persons in any given situation.

e. Provides awareness activities designed to   0 1 2 3 4 5
sensitize nondisabled students to the prob-
lems and feelings of their handicapped peers
and to help break down attitudinal barriers.

f. Provides opportunities for disabled students   0 1 2 3 4 5
to discuss their disabilities either formally or
informally.

C { Scale: 0-not yet attempted 1-beginning planning 2-advanced planning
3-beginning implementation 4-partial implementation 5-advanced implementation

Letters refer to example in Figure 2, below.

Next to each goal statement you will find a score sheet.

E On the score sheet record your rating for each item.

F Multiply the rating by the weight factor as shown.

The weight factor is a determination of the amount of effort it takes to fully implement an item. Effort entails such factors as: time, money, staff, staff coordination, and/or convenience.

1—minimal effort   2—average effort   3—extensive effort

G This will determine your item score.

H Add all the item scores to find the total.

I Divide the total item scores by the number indicated to find the average goal score (AGS). Round off to the nearest tenth.

After you have calculated all your average goal scores, proceed to "Graph Profile," page 192.

Figure 2

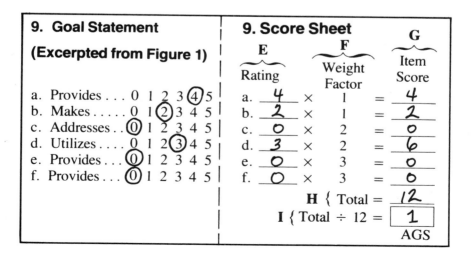

RATING SCALE KEY ("SCALE")

0 - Not yet attempted. You have done nothing of concrete substance (although others, such as special education teachers or classroom teachers, may perform the task).

1 - Beginning planning. You are planning to do this (e.g., you have taken steps to gather materials, consulted with resources people, identified areas of need, etc.).

2 - Advanced planning. You have developed a plan to do this but have not yet started (i.e., you have defined goals and developed plans and activities).

3 - Beginning implementation. You have just begun to do this (i.e., you have begun to carry out some activities and plans).

4 - Partial implementation. You are doing this sometimes, in some situations but not all—or you are doing this to some degree (e.g., you are in the process of carrying out evaluations, or you are revising plans and activities).

5 - Advanced implementation. You consistently do this in all cases (i.e., you are implementing all of the plans and activities; and you continually evaluate, update, and further develop plans and activities to meet changing needs).

1. Goal Statement (Staffing—Professional Competencies)

The media specialist is familiar with the mandates of federal and state legislation relating to disabled people and the implications of these mandates for the media center program.

The media specialist:

1. Score Sheet

	Rating						Weight Factor	Item Score

a. Reads about the laws and becomes familiar with the disabling conditions which the laws cover.   0 1 2 3 4 5

a. _____ × 1 = _____

b. Reviews and/or studies materials (e.g., articles, books, etc.) about specific disabling conditions, PL 94-142, mainstreaming, etc.   0 1 2 3 4 5

b. _____ × 2 = _____

c. Reviews and studies the building and/or district plans to implement federal and state mandates.   0 1 2 3 4 5

c. _____ × 3 = _____

Total = _____

Total ÷ 6 = ☐ AGS

Scale: 0-not yet attempted 1-beginning planning 2-advanced planning 3-beginning implementation 4-partial implementation 5-advanced implementation

2. Score Sheet

The media specialist utilizes external sources to access information and materials on PL 94-142, disabling conditions, mainstreaming, etc.

The media specialist:

	Rating	Weight Factor	Item Score
a. Develops a system for identifying and accessing external resources. Such resources might include any or all of the following—computer-based indexes, school districts, regional education districts, state departments of education, universities and colleges, state libraries and the Library of Congress's National Library Services for the Blind and Physically Handicapped, professional education and library associations (media, special education, vocational education, etc.), government and private agencies and organizations, individuals (special educators, disabled persons, etc.), and organizations of disabled persons.	0 1 2 3 4 5	a. _____ × 2 =	_____
b. Uses the various external resources mentioned above.	0 1 2 3 4 5	b. _____ × 3 =	
		Total =	_____
		Total ÷ 5 =	☐ AGS

Scale: 0-not yet attempted 1-beginning planning 2-advanced planning 3-beginning implementation 4-partial implementation 5-advanced implementation

3. Goal Statement (Staffing—Personal Competencies)

The media specialist demonstrates a commitment to the ideas of mainstreaming through personal attitudes and actions.

The media specialist:

a. Actively invites and welcomes all disabled students into the media center.　0 1 2 3 4 5

b. Is conscious of stigmatic terminology and does not use such terms to label disabled people.　0 1 2 3 4 5

c. Communicates and interacts with disabled and nondisabled students on an equal basis, both formally and informally.　0 1 2 3 4 5

d. Recognizes that body language is a means of communication and works on controlling gestures, expressions, etc. which convey negative feelings.　0 1 2 3 4 5

e. Consults with disabled students, special educators, parents, and others about ways to promote understanding about disabled people.　0 1 2 3 4 5

3. Score Sheet

	Rating	Weight Factor	Item Score
a.	___	× 1 =	___
b.	___	× 1 =	___
c.	___	× 1 =	___
d.	___	× 2 =	___
e.	___	× 3 =	___
		Total =	___
		Total ÷ 8 =	☐ AGS

Scale: 0-not yet attempted 1-beginning planning 2-advanced planning 3-beginning implementation 4-partial implementation 5-advanced implementation

4. Goal Statement (Staffing—Managing)

The media specialist accepts responsibility for seeing that the entire media center staff, both paid and volunteer, express themselves positively in relation to disabled students.

The media specialist:

a. Works with disabled students along with and/or in front of the rest of the media center staff.   0 1 2 3 4 5

b. Encourages and expects media center aides and volunteers to work with all students.   0 1 2 3 4 5

c. Observes and evaluates the media center staff to see that they are demonstrating such behaviors as sensitivity, patience, and equal acceptance of all students.   0 1 2 3 4 5

d. Provides media center staff with informational materials and resources (e.g., related workshops and classes) to help them work more effectively with disabled students.   0 1 2 3 4 5

e. Provides media center staff with personal assistance to increase their skills and to make their contact with disabled students easier and more effective.   0 1 2 3 4 5

f. Coordinates inservice programs for media center staff to assist them in working with disabled students.   0 1 2 3 4 5

g. Includes media staff in school- and districtwide inservice programs dealing with mainstreaming topics.   0 1 2 3 4 5

h. Assigns media staff special tasks to use their talents and interests in working with disabled students.   0 1 2 3 4 5

Scale: 0-not yet attempted 1-beginning planning 2-advanced planning 3-beginning implementation 4-partial implementation 5-advanced implementation

4. Score Sheet

	Rating	Weight Factor	Item Score
a.	____	× 1 =	____
b.	____	× 1 =	____
c.	____	× 1 =	____
d.	____	× 2 =	____
e.	____	× 2 =	____
f.	____	× 2 =	____
g.	____	× 3 =	____
h.	____	× 3 =	____
		Total =	____
		Total ÷ 15 =	____

AGS

5. Goal Statement (Staffing—Managing)

The media specialist develops a media student aide program which contributes positively to the media center environment and philosophy of service for all students.

The media specialist:

a. Provides student helpers with instruction about media center policies and procedures and their responsibility in creating a positive environment for all students. 0 1 2 3 4 5

b. Recruits disabled students as student helpers. 0 1 2 3 4 5

c. Assigns tasks on the basis of interest, aptitude, and potential ability to perform the tasks. 0 1 2 3 4 5

d. Trains students for tasks they are to perform, adapting training techniques for disabled students when necessary. 0 1 2 3 4 5

e. Provides student helpers with activities aimed at developing understanding about similarities and differences among individuals. 0 1 2 3 4 5

f. Provides student helpers with training in special techniques for assisting disabled students in using materials and services. 0 1 2 3 4 5

5. Score Sheet

	Rating	Weight Factor	Item Score
a.	___	× 1 =	___
b.	___	× 1 =	___
c.	___	× 1 =	___
d.	___	× 2 =	___
e.	___	× 2 =	___
f.	___	× 3 =	___

Total = ___

Total ÷ 10 = [___] AGS

Scale: 0-not yet attempted 1-beginning planning 2-advanced planning 3-beginning implementation 4-partial implementation 5-advanced implementation

6. Goal Statement (Staffing—Resource to Teachers)

The media specialist cooperates with classroom teachers to help them identify and select media resources for teaching disabled students.

The media specialist:

a. Responds to specific requests from teachers for media resources for disabled students.   0 1 2 3 4 5

b. Communicates that the role of the media specialist includes working cooperatively with teachers in the area of media resources for disabled students.   0 1 2 3 4 5

c. Updates self regarding curriculum developments and instructional design for disabled students.   0 1 2 3 4 5

d. Employs a record-keeping system to note teacher interests, plans, needs, etc. for teaching disabled students and informs them of new resources to use.   0 1 2 3 4 5

e. Initiates a system within the school to identify new and varied uses for the building collection in meeting the needs of disabled students.   0 1 2 3 4 5

6. Score Sheet

Rating	Weight Factor	Item Score
a. ___	× 1 =	___
b. ___	× 1 =	___
c. ___	× 2 =	___
d. ___	× 3 =	___
e. ___	× 3 =	___
	Total =	___
	Total ÷ 10 =	[___] AGS

Scale: 0-not yet attempted 1-beginning planning 2-advanced planning 3-beginning implementation 4-partial implementation 5-advanced implementation

7. Goal Statement (Staffing—Resource to Teachers)

The media specialist builds and maintains a professional library collection for teachers and staff which includes materials related to mainstreaming.

The media specialist:

a. Maintains an accessible, up-to-date, and diverse professional collection including media and special education books, journals, and newsletters. 0 1 2 3 4 5

b. Places name on mailing lists to receive publications from various organizations serving the disabled. 0 1 2 3 4 5

c. Circulates materials on the disabled to teachers (e.g., lists of new materials, or relevant articles). 0 1 2 3 4 5

d. Requests suggestions from teachers, staff, and others for additional materials on mainstreaming to add to the professional collection. 0 1 2 3 4 5

e. Develops an efficient system of obtaining teachers' recommendations for items and for sharing information with other teachers about specific suggestions for use with disabled students. 0 1 2 3 4 5

f. Develops and distributes bibliographies on mainstreaming, etc. 0 1 2 3 4 5

g. Asks special educators to review special education materials and note their applicability and usefulness for other teachers. 0 1 2 3 4 5

Scale: 0-not yet attempted 1-beginning planning 2-advanced planning 3-beginning implementation 4-partial implementation 5-advanced implementation

7. Score Sheet

Rating	Weight Factor	Item Score
a. _____	× 1 =	_____
b. _____	× 1 =	_____
c. _____	× 2 =	_____
d. _____	× 2 =	_____
e. _____	× 3 =	_____
f. _____	× 3 =	_____
g. _____	× 3 =	_____
	Total =	_____
	Total ÷ 15 =	_____ AGS

8. Goal Statement (Staffing—Resource to Teachers)

The media specialist offers support to school administrators in promoting mainstreaming.

The media specialist:

a. Responds to the principal's requests for information on mainstreaming and disabling conditions.   0 1 2 3 4 5

b. Includes administrators in the system in circulating professional materials.   0 1 2 3 4 5

c. Circulates materials received by administrators.   0 1 2 3 4 5

d. Informs administration about the needs of the media center program in accommodating disabled students, and the success of mainstreaming in the media center.   0 1 2 3 4 5

8. Score Sheet

Rating	Weight Factor	Item Score
a. ____	× 1 =	____
b. ____	× 1 =	____
c. ____	× 2 =	____
d. ____	× 2 =	____
	Total =	____
	Total ÷ 6 =	☐ AGS

Scale: 0-not yet attempted 1-beginning planning 2-advanced planning 3-beginning implementation 4-partial implementation 5-advanced implementation

9. Goal Statement (Staffing—Students)

The media specialist helps nondisabled students to communicate and relate positively to disabled students.

The media specialist:

a. Provides informational materials about disabling conditions. 0 1 2 3 4 5

b. Makes media available (fiction, nonfiction, print, nonprint) which present a positive, fair, and balanced representation of disabled persons. 0 1 2 3 4 5

c. Addresses attitudinal changes through literature, films, speakers, and experiential activities. 0 1 2 3 4 5

d. Utilizes materials that accustom students to seeing, hearing, and reading about disabled persons in any given situation. 0 1 2 3 4 5

e. Provides awareness activities designed to sensitize nondisabled students to the problems and feelings of their disabled peers and to help break down attitudinal barriers. 0 1 2 3 4 5

f. Provides opportunities for disabled students to discuss their disabilities either formally or informally. 0 1 2 3 4 5

9. Score Sheet

Rating	Weight Factor	Item Score
a. ____	× 1 =	____
b. ____	× 1 =	____
c. ____	× 2 =	____
d. ____	× 2 =	____
e. ____	× 3 =	____
f. ____	× 3 =	____
	Total =	____
	Total ÷ 12 =	____ AGS

Scale: 0-not yet attempted 1-beginning planning 2-advanced planning 3-beginning implementation 4-partial implementation 5-advanced implementation

10. Goal Statement (Staffing—Students)

The media specialist makes provisions to include disabled students in all media center activities.

The media specialist:

a. Conducts a flexible program to meet the needs of disabled and nondisabled students.   0 1 2 3 4 5

b. Provides multisensory experiences using a wide range of materials and formats.   0 1 2 3 4 5

c. Provides hands-on experiences and activities which encourage self-expression.   0 1 2 3 4 5

d. Varies the lengths of activities and provides options for participation.   0 1 2 3 4 5

e. Designs activities in which disabled students also have opportunities to assume leadership roles and/or take their turns in being the center of activity.   0 1 2 3 4 5

f. Employs rules which are simple, clear and consistent, and applicable to disabled students as well as to nondisabled students.   0 1 2 3 4 5

Scale: 0-not yet attempted 1-beginning planning 2-advanced planning 3-beginning implementation 4-partial implementation 5-advanced implementation

10. Score Sheet

	Rating	Weight Factor		Item Score
a.	_____	× 1	=	_____
b.	_____	× 1	=	_____
c.	_____	× 1	=	_____
d.	_____	× 1	=	_____
e.	_____	× 1	=	_____
f.	_____	× 1	=	_____

10. Goal Statement (Staffing—Students) (continued)

g. Designs activities where success and participation are not prevented by a specific disability and which stress cooperation rather than individual competition.

0 1 2 3 4 5

h. Involves disabled and nondisabled students in the development of media center rules and procedures.

0 1 2 3 4 5

i. Familiarizes self with safety procedures for disabled students using the media center (evacuation, special safety considerations, etc.).

0 1 2 3 4 5

j. Plans and makes arrangements for media center activities well in advance so that disabled students can be accommodated (e.g., physical access to buildings and rooms, transportation, and seating).

0 1 2 3 4 5

k. Assesses need and arranges for special materials, equipment, and supplies for disabled students to use in participating in special activities.

0 1 2 3 4 5

	Rating	Weight Factor	Item Score
g.	____	× 2 =	____
h.	____	× 2 =	____
i.	____	× 2 =	____
j.	____	× 3 =	____
k.	____	× 3 =	____
		Total =	____
		Total ÷ 18 =	☐ AGS

Scale: 0-not yet attempted 1-beginning planning 2-advanced planning 3-beginning implementation 4-partial implementation 5-advanced implementation

11. Goal Statement (Staffing—Community)

The media specialist takes advantage of the many resources in the community for working with disabled individuals.

The media specialist:

a. Identifies persons or groups who have information and skills in working with disabled individuals.   0 1 2 3 4 5

b. Keeps a media center file of the human and other resources available in the community.   0 1 2 3 4 5

c. Establishes programs to bring disabled adults into the school to serve as positive role models for students.   0 1 2 3 4 5

d. Involves parents of disabled students in informational forums and informal discussions.   0 1 2 3 4 5

e. Establishes a media center community advisory committee which includes disabled persons and/or parents of disabled students.   0 1 2 3 4 5

Scale: 0-not yet attempted 1-beginning planning 2-advanced planning 3-beginning implementation 4-partial implementation 5-advanced implementation

11. Score Sheet

Rating	Weight Factor	Item Score
a. _____	× 1 =	_____
b. _____	× 2 =	_____
c. _____	× 2 =	_____
d. _____	× 2 =	_____
e. _____	× 3 =	_____
	Total =	_____
	Total ÷ 10 =	☐ AGS

12. Goal Statement (Services—Processing)

The media specialist processes and catalogs materials in ways that make them usable and accessible for students with specific disabling conditions.

The media specialist:

a. Develops packaging which allows easier retrieval and accessibility (handles and loops on boxes, special labels, etc.).   0 1 2 3 4 5

b. Evaluates incoming materials, adapting them to meet special needs (spirally binds materials to lay flat for students with dexterity problems, laminates, reinforces, etc.).   0 1 2 3 4 5

c. Provides varying formats for sections of the catalog as needed, such as a large print listing of large print books for visually impaired students.   0 1 2 3 4 5

d. Regularly checks and repairs all materials and equipment which show wear and damage that could hinder effective usage by disabled students.   0 1 2 3 4 5

12. Score Sheet

Rating	Weight Factor	Item Score
a. _____	× 2 =	_____
b. _____	× 3 =	_____
c. _____	× 3 =	_____
d. _____	× 3 =	_____
	Total =	_____

Total ÷ 11 = ☐ AGS

Scale: 0-not yet attempted 1-beginning planning 2-advanced planning 3-beginning implementation 4-partial implementation 5-advanced implementation

13. Goal Statement (Services—Circulation)

The media specialist modifies the circulation sytem to eliminate procedures which might be barriers to disabled students.

The media specialist:

a. Develops and/or adapts simplified circulation procedures.   0 1 2 3 4 5

b. Removes limitations on use of materials which restrict usage by some disabled students: length of time materials can be checked out; number of items allowed checked out at one time; types of materials that can be checked out; and schedule of times for checking out materials and equipment.   0 1 2 3 4 5

13. Score Sheet

Rating	Weight Factor	Item Score
a. _____	× 2 =	_____
b. _____	× 2 =	_____
	Total =	_____
	Total ÷ 4 =	☐ AGS

Scale: 0-not yet attempted 1-beginning planning 2-advanced planning 3-beginning implementation 4-partial implementation 5-advanced implementation

14. Goal Statement (Services—Reference)

The media specialist considers the specific needs and limitations of each disabled student in using the media center's reference collection and services.

The media specialist:

a. Is available and approachable to assist disabled students to use   0 1 2 3 4 5
   the reference collection and service.

b. Informs disabled students about the network of reference ser-   0 1 2 3 4 5
   vices available outside the school, such as the school district,
   public libraries, special libraries, governmental agencies,
   museums, human resources, and library networks.

c. Pairs students to facilitate use of cumbersome or difficult refer-   0 1 2 3 4 5
   ence materials.

14. Score Sheet

	Rating	Weight Factor	Item Score
a.	_____	× 1 =	_____
b.	_____	× 2 =	_____
c.	_____	× 2 =	_____
		Total =	_____
		Total ÷ 5 =	☐ AGS

Scale: 0-not yet attempted 1-beginning planning 2-advanced planning 3-beginning implementation 4-partial implementation 5-advanced implementation

15. Goal Statements (Services—Inservices)

The media specialist cooperates with special educators and school administrators as they plan and organize teacher inservice programs related to mainstreaming in the classroom and the media center.

The media specialist:

a. Determines the need and builds support for teacher inservice programs by assessing whether teachers encourage and plan for use of the media center by disabled students.   0 1 2 3 4 5

b. Determines the need and builds support for teacher inservice programs by assessing teacher requests for media center materials and assistance in working with disabled students.   0 1 2 3 4 5

c. Plans and implements inservice programs as part of the media center program to present new media center materials, specialized equipment, adaptation techniques, etc. for disabled students.   0 1 2 3 4 5

d. Assists with schoolwide teacher inservice programs on mainstreaming by providing materials, equipment, and space and by arranging for speakers, etc.   0 1 2 3 4 5

Scale: 0-not yet attempted 1-beginning planning 2-advanced planning 3-beginning implementation 4-partial implementation 5-advanced implementation

15. Score Sheet

	Rating	Weight Factor	Item Score
a.	_____	× 1 =	_____
b.	_____	× 1 =	_____
c.	_____	× 3 =	_____
d.	_____	× 3 =	_____
		Total =	_____
		Total ÷ 8 =	_____ AGS

16. Goal Statement (Services—Production)

The media specialist develops a media center program for the design, production, and adaptation of materials for disabled students.

The media specialist:

a. Provides facilities, equipment, and supplies for use by teachers, students, and aides in producing or adapting materials for disabled students.

0 1 2 3 4 5

b. Assesses the need for producing or adapting materials by determining availability of products through the school, outside resources, or commercial sources.

0 1 2 3 4 5

c. Researches ways of adapting materials for special needs.

0 1 2 3 4 5

d. Arranges instruction to train teachers, students, and aides in production skills for developing and adapting materials.

0 1 2 3 4 5

e. Develops production services for adapting materials for disabled students (such as videotaping demonstrations and transferring written material to other formats).

0 1 2 3 4 5

f. Designs and produces instructional materials in consultation with special education and classroom teachers.

0 1 2 3 4 5

g. Takes workshops, courses, and participates in inservice programs to learn new techniques for adapting materials for special needs.

0 1 2 3 4 5

Scale: 0-not yet attempted 1-beginning planning 2-advanced planning 3-beginning implementation 4-partial implementation 5-advanced implementation

16. Score Sheet

	Rating	Weight Factor	Item Score
a.	_____	× 1 =	_____
b.	_____	× 2 =	_____
c.	_____	× 2 =	_____
d.	_____	× 2 =	_____
e.	_____	× 3 =	_____
f.	_____	× 3 =	_____
g.	_____	× 3 =	_____
		Total =	_____
		Total ÷ 16 =	[___] AGS

17. Goal Statement (Services—Public Relations)

The media specialist publicizes the media center in the school and community to foster interest, participation, and support for mainstreaming in the media center.

The media specialist:

a. Disseminates news items, lists of new materials, announcements of upcoming events, including those relevant to disabled students, through student newspapers and take-home flyers.   0 1 2 3 4 5

b. Incorporates a sound mainstreaming philosophy in all media center displays and bulletin boards (e.g., provides a fair representation of disabled persons and a variety of formats in response to specific needs).   0 1 2 3 4 5

c. Publicizes through local news media special media center activities, including those involving disabled students.   0 1 2 3 4 5

d. Sponsors programs, such as open houses and forums, which educate the public about mainstreaming.   0 1 2 3 4 5

17. Score Sheet

Rating	Weight Factor	Item Score
a. _____	× 1 =	_____
b. _____	× 2 =	_____
c. _____	× 3 =	_____
d. _____	× 3 =	_____
	Total =	_____
	Total ÷ 9 =	☐ AGS

Scale: 0-not yet attempted 1-beginning planning 2-advanced planning 3-beginning implementation 4-partial implementation 5-advanced implementation

18. Goal Statement (Services—Orientation)

The media specialist designs media center orientation activities to include disabled students.

The media specialist:

a. Incorporates varied formats and presentation methods into regular orientation, so that separate sessions designed for disabled students are not so necessary.   0 1 2 3 4 5

b. Obtains suggestions from classroom and special education teachers on adapting orientation methods to meet the needs of disabled students.   0 1 2 3 4 5

c. Observes disabled students and notes individual need for practice and repetition, providing assistance individually and informally as part of everyday service.   0 1 2 3 4 5

d. Organizes orientation so that it is an *ongoing systematic service,* rather than an annual event.   0 1 2 3 4 5

e. Individualizes orientation activities and materials to accommodate needs of the disabled student.   0 1 2 3 4 5

f. Organizes and mediates orientation information to make it available at all times for individual reference.   0 1 2 3 4 5

g. Designs media center guides and handbooks in various formats.   0 1 2 3 4 5

Scale: 0-not yet attempted 1-beginning planning 2-advanced planning 3-beginning implementation 4-partial implementation 5-advanced implementation

18. Score Sheet

Rating	Weight Factor	Item Score
a. _____	× 2 =	_____
b. _____	× 2 =	_____
c. _____	× 2 =	_____
d. _____	× 2 =	_____
e. _____	× 3 =	_____
f. _____	× 3 =	_____
g. _____	× 3 =	_____
	Total =	_____
	Total ÷ 17 =	_____

AGS

19. Goal Statement (Instruction)

The media specialist acknowledges the influence of specific disabling conditions on individual ability, rate of learning, and learning style.

The media specialist:

a. Consults with special education teachers regarding the degree of impairment for the individual student and the affect of that impairment on learning.   0 1 2 3 4 5

b. Identifies instructional needs which are common to both disabled and nondisabled students.   0 1 2 3 4 5

c. Modifies environmental, social, and physical conditions to enhance learning situations for disabled students.   0 1 2 3 4 5

d. Designs instructional programs for an individual disabled student's specific learning problems, based on known principles and theories of learning.   0 1 2 3 4 5

19. Score Sheet

Rating	Weight Factor	Item Score
a.	_____ × 2 =	_____
b.	_____ × 2 =	_____
c.	_____ × 3 =	_____
d.	_____ × 3 =	_____
	Total =	_____
	Total ÷ 10 =	☐ AGS

Scale: 0-not yet attempted 1-beginning planning 2-advanced planning 3-beginning implementation 4-partial implementation 5-advanced implementation

20. Goal Statement (Instruction—Classroom)

The media specialist cooperatively designs and assists in the implementation of classroom instruction for disabled students.

The media specialist:

a. Becomes familiar with school and district curriculum programs in which disabled students are included.   0 1 2 3 4 5

b. Keeps abreast of classroom instructional programs in which disabled students are included.   0 1 2 3 4 5

c. Works with teachers on instructional design for the classroom to accommodate the needs of disabled students.   0 1 2 3 4 5

d. Mediates classroom instruction through identifying and selecting appropriate instructional media and equipment and by helping to produce special instructional materials.   0 1 2 3 4 5

e. Contributes to the design, development, and implementation of IEPs (Individualized Education Programs).   0 1 2 3 4 5

20. Score Sheet

	Rating	Weight Factor	Item Score
a.	___	× 1 =	___
b.	___	× 1 =	___
c.	___	× 3 =	___
d.	___	× 3 =	___
e.	___	× 3 =	___
		Total =	___

Total ÷ 11 = ☐ AGS

Scale: 0-not yet attempted 1-beginning planning 2-advanced planning 3-beginning implementation 4-partial implementation 5-advanced implementation

21. Goal Statement (Instruction—Media Skills)

In cooperation with classroom and special education teachers, the media specialist develops a program of media skills instruction to accommodate the needs of disabled students.

The media specialist:

a. Identifies, adapts, or designs formal and informal assessment tools/methods to determine disabled students' strengths and weaknesses in all media skills areas.   0 1 2 3 4 5

b. Uses assessment methods with groups and/or individual disabled students to determine media skills instructional needs.   0 1 2 3 4 5

c. Designs media skills instruction using specific teaching techniques, equipment and materials, based on the assessed needs of disabled students.   0 1 2 3 4 5

d. Integrates the media skills instruction with relevant curriculum content being taught to disabled students in the classroom.   0 1 2 3 4 5

21. Score Sheet

Rating	Weight Factor	Item Score
a. _____	× 2 =	_____
b. _____	× 2 =	_____
c. _____	× 3 =	_____
d. _____	× 3 =	_____
	Total =	_____
	Total ÷ 10 =	☐ AGS

Scale: 0-not yet attempted 1-beginning planning 2-advanced planning 3-beginning implementation 4-partial implementation 5-advanced implementation

22. Score Sheet

	Rating	Weight Factor	Item Score
a.	____	× 1 =	____
b.	____	× 1 =	____
c.	____	× 1 =	____
d.	____	× 1 =	____
e.	____	× 1 =	____
f.	____	× 2 =	____
g.	____	× 2 =	____
h.	____	× 2 =	____
i.	____	× 2 =	____
		Total =	____
		Total ÷ 13 =	[ ] AGS

22. Goal Statement (Instruction—Techniques)

The media specialist uses instructional techniques which enhance learning for disabled and nondisabled students alike.

The media specialist:

a. Arranges seating and setting for instructional activities which will enhance learning and minimize distractions and limitations caused by disabilities.   0 1 2 3 4 5

b. Uses a variety of instructional formats and materials which meet specific needs of disabled students.   0 1 2 3 4 5

c. Uses demonstration as a technique whenever possible, allowing students to assist in demonstrations.   0 1 2 3 4 5

d. Provides hands-on opportunities for student involvement before and after demonstrations.   0 1 2 3 4 5

e. Encourages appropriate participation (by asking questions, offering assistance in demonstrations, etc.).   0 1 2 3 4 5

f. Individualizes instruction and allows the student's rate of learning to direct the pace of instructional activities and practice.   0 1 2 3 4 5

g. Maintains a balance of group and individual work, minimizing competition and maximizing cooperation.   0 1 2 3 4 5

h. Finds ways to take advantage of students' strengths and to enhance learning through structures such as pairing, small cooperative groups, and tutoring.   0 1 2 3 4 5

i. Applies a variety of techniques using standard equipment and materials to meet specific instructional needs of disabled students.   0 1 2 3 4 5

Scale: 0-not yet attempted 1-beginning planning 2-advanced planning 3-beginning implementation 4-partial implementation 5-advanced implementation

23. Goal Statement (Instruction—Personal Style)

The media specialist develops a personal teaching style that enhances learning for disabled and nondisabled students alike.

The media specialist:

a. Seeks ways to analyze personal teaching style and to make improvements as necessary (e.g., has self videotaped to assess communication effectiveness).   0 1 2 3 4 5

b. Makes a conscious effort to improve voice quality, projection, vocabulary, etc., as necessary.   0 1 2 3 4 5

c. Gives directions which are concise, precise but comprehensive, using a variety of formats.   0 1 2 3 4 5

d. Weighs the advantages of using specific teaching techniques against the disadvantages, e.g., using equipment versus using personal contact and reinforcement; using tutors versus using teacher contact; or small group versus one-to-one activities.   0 1 2 3 4 5

23. Score Sheet

	Weight	Item
Rating	Factor	Score

a. _____ × 2 = _____

b. _____ × 2 = _____

c. _____ × 2 = _____

d. _____ × 2 = _____

Total = _____

Total ÷ 8 = [___] AGS

Scale: 0-not yet attempted 1-beginning planning 2-advanced planning 3-beginning implementation 4-partial implementation 5-advanced implementation

24. Goal Statement (Collection—Inventory)

The media specialist knows what materials (print and nonprint) are available for use by and for disabled students in the media center, the school, and the district support systems.

The media specialist:

a. Coordinates the inventory and cataloging of all media within the school.

0 1 2 3 4 5

b. Keeps up-to-date listings of media available through district and regional centers.

0 1 2 3 4 5

c. Consults with special education teachers to assess the media needs of disabled students in relation to the collection.

0 1 2 3 4 5

d. Evaluates the collection in terms of quality and usability by disabled students and their teachers.

0 1 2 3 4 5

24. Score Sheet

	Rating	Weight Factor	Item Score
a.	_____	× 2 =	_____
b.	_____	× 2 =	_____
c.	_____	× 2 =	_____
d.	_____	× 3 =	_____

Total = _____

Total ÷ 9 = [____] AGS

Scale: 0-not yet attempted 1-beginning planning 2-advanced planning 3-beginning implementation 4-partial implementation 5-advanced implementation

25. Goal Statement (Collection—Evaluation and Selection)

The media specialist involves disabled students and those who work with them in the evaluation and selection of materials and equipment.

The media specialist:

a. Encourages staff and student participation in the evaluation and selection of materials for disabled students.   0 1 2 3 4 5

b. Sets up a system for regular preview and assessment of materials which involves disabled students, teachers, and staff, to ensure that disabled students' needs are being met.   0 1 2 3 4 5

c. Develops a selection policy which reflects the needs of disabled students as to format, quality, content, and quantity of media center materials, as well as a concern for fair representation of disabled persons in the materials.   0 1 2 3 4 5

Scale: 0-not yet attempted 1-beginning planning 2-advanced planning 3-beginning implementation 4-partial implementation 5-advanced implementation

25. Score Sheet

Rating	Weight Factor	Item Score
a. _____	× 1 =	_____
b. _____	× 3 =	_____
c. _____	× 3 =	_____
	Total =	_____

Total ÷ 7 = [ ] AGS

26. Goal Statement (Collection—IEP Development)

The media specialist works with special educators and other school staff in developing and implementing individualized education programs (IEPs).

The media specialist:

a. Provides information to IEP teams concerning availability of materials and equipment for implementing specific goals and objectives.   0 1 2 3 4 5

b. Conveys personal experience and knowledge regarding diversified usage of standard materials and equipment to meet disabled students' needs.   0 1 2 3 4 5

c. Informs teams about innovative materials and equipment being developed for use with disabled students.   0 1 2 3 4 5

d. Actively participates on IEP teams.   0 1 2 3 4 5

26. Score Sheet

Rating	Weight Factor	Item Score
a. _____	× 2 =	_____
b. _____	× 2 =	_____
c. _____	× 2 =	_____
d. _____	× 3 =	_____
	Total =	_____
	Total ÷ 9 =	☐ AGS

Scale: 0-not yet attempted 1-beginning planning 2-advanced planning 3-beginning implementation 4-partial implementation 5-advanced implementation

27. Goal Statement (Collection—Availability)

The media specialist is familiar with sources for borrowing and funding special materials and equipment for disabled students.

The media specialist:

a. Is familiar with local sources for borrowing specialized materials and equipment.   0 1 2 3 4 5

b. Consults with special education and classroom teachers regarding additional sources at regional and national levels.   0 1 2 3 4 5

c. Keeps files of sources for specific material and equipment needs for disabled students (including addresses, specifications, qualifications for usage, restrictions, etc.)   0 1 2 3 4 5

d. Sets up cooperative agreements with other media centers and organizations for borrowing and/or sharing specialized materials and equipment.   0 1 2 3 4 5

e. Becomes familiar with and makes contacts with organizations which will fund special needs (service clubs, government programs, churches, etc.)   0 1 2 3 4 5

Scale: 0-not yet attempted 1-beginning planning 2-advanced planning 3-beginning implementation 4-partial implementation 5-advanced implementation

27. Score Sheet

	Rating	Weight Factor	Item Score
a.	___	× 2 =	___
b.	___	× 2 =	___
c.	___	× 2 =	___
d.	___	× 3 =	___
e.	___	× 3 =	___
		Total =	___
		Total ÷ 12 =	___ AGS

28. Goal Statement (Equipment—Standard)

The media specialist provides a variety of standard equipment for use by disabled students and staff who work with them.

The media specialist:

a. Tests standard equipment to assess specific difficulties and limitations in operation by disabled students. 0 1 2 3 4 5

b. Weighs the advantage of using audiovisual equipment against the need for personal contact and reinforcement and decides when one approach is more appropriate than another. 0 1 2 3 4 5

c. Consults with special education and other resource people to develop innovative ways to use and adapt standard equipment. 0 1 2 3 4 5

d. Designs instruction and activities based on creative use of standard equipment. 0 1 2 3 4 5

e. Acquires new equipment through borrowing or purchasing to meet the needs of disabled students when existing standard equipment cannot be adapted. 0 1 2 3 4 5

28. Score Sheet

	Rating	Weight Factor	Item Score
a.	_____	× 2 =	_____
b.	_____	× 2 =	_____
c.	_____	× 3 =	_____
d.	_____	× 3 =	_____
e.	_____	× 3 =	_____
		Total =	_____
		Total ÷ 13 =	[ ] AGS

Scale: 0-not yet attempted 1-beginning planning 2-advanced planning 3-beginning implementation 4-partial implementation 5-advanced implementation

29. Goal Statement (Equipment—Specialized)

The media specialist works with special education teachers to determine specialized equipment needs for individual disabled students.

The media specialist:

a. Provides storage for and easy access to specialized equipment needed in the media center for use by disabled students.   0 1 2 3 4 5

b. Consults with special education teachers concerning usage limitations of specialized equipment and why particular students need specific equipment.   0 1 2 3 4 5

c. Is able to use and operate specialized equipment.   0 1 2 3 4 5

d. Designs instructional activities, in cooperation with special educators, based on the creative use of specialized equipment.   0 1 2 3 4 5

29. Score Sheet

	Rating	Weight Factor	Item Score
a.	_____	× 1 =	_____
b.	_____	× 2 =	_____
c.	_____	× 2 =	_____
d.	_____	× 3 =	_____
		Total =	_____

Total ÷ 8 = ☐ AGS

Scale: 0-not yet attempted 1-beginning planning 2-advanced planning 3-beginning implementation 4-partial implementation 5-advanced implementation

30. Goal Statement (Facilities and Environment)

The media specialist works with the school principal and other appropriate personnel to assure that the media center and its programs are fully accessible and meet the standards of Section 504 of PL 93-112 (Rehabilitation Act).

The media specialist:

a. Assesses the media center in terms of its physical accessibility to all students in accordance with the mandates of Section 504 of PL 93-112.   0 1 2 3 4 5

b. Asks disabled students to help analyze what physical barriers exist for them *in* the media center.   0 1 2 3 4 5

c. Consults publications about barrier-free access to and within buildings.   0 1 2 3 4 5

d. Initiates actions to bring about compliance with the law in order to accommodate disabled students in the media center and its programs.   0 1 2 3 4 5

30. Score Sheet

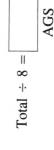

Rating	Weight Factor	Item Score
a. _____	× 1 =	_____
b. _____	× 2 =	_____
c. _____	× 2 =	_____
d. _____	× 3 =	_____
	Total =	_____
	Total ÷ 8 =	☐ AGS

Scale: 0-not yet attempted 1-beginning planning 2-advanced planning 3-beginning implementation 4-partial implementation 5-advanced implementation

31. Goal Statement (Facilities and Environment)

The media specialist develops a media center environment which meets disabled students' diverse needs for personal comfort, security, and learning enhancement.

The media specialist:

a. Designs a variety of spaces to accommodate the wide range of learning activities of disabled and nondisabled students in the media center (e.g., areas for quiet individual study, group work, equipment usage, leisure activities, and production). 0 1 2 3 4 5

b. Enhances the media center environment through creative use of color, design, lighting, sound, etc., in an attempt to make disabled students feel welcome. 0 1 2 3 4 5

c. Provides furniture for disabled students which is comfortable, as well as functional and accessible. 0 1 2 3 4 5

d. Consults with special education teachers to determine special lighting, sound, and other environmental needs of individual disabled students. 0 1 2 3 4 5

e. Provides technical furnishings (circulation desk, card catalog, shelving, etc.) which are accessible and usable by disabled students. 0 1 2 3 4 5

Scale: 0-not yet attempted 1-beginning planning 2-advanced planning 3-beginning implementation 4-partial implementation 5-advanced implementation

31. Score Sheet

Rating	Weight Factor	Item Score
a. _____	× 1 =	_____
b. _____	× 2 =	_____
c. _____	× 2 =	_____
d. _____	× 3 =	_____
e. _____	× 3 =	_____
	Total =	_____
	Total ÷ 11 =	[ ] AGS

The following goal statements and indicators relate to *specific disabilities*. If you do not have students in your school with a particular specific disability, mark "0" on the AGS for that goal statement.

32. Goal Statement (Learning-Disabled Students)

The media specialist develops media center programs responsive to the special needs of learning-disabled students.

The media specialist:

a. Reads and studies information about learning disabilities.　0 1 2 3 4 5

b. Uses a variety of formats to instruct, practice, review, and test.　0 1 2 3 4 5

c. Provides opportunities for students to make choices of activities and ways of responding.　0 1 2 3 4 5

d. Designs instructional activities which accommodate the individual student's specific learning disability.　0 1 2 3 4 5

e. Consults with special education and classroom teachers, parents, students or others concerning—individual learning styles, strengths/weaknesses, habits/interests, special equipment/material needs, social behavior patterns, degree of impairment/limitations, problems with socialization, and suggested approaches for reaching the student.　0 1 2 3 4 5

32. Score Sheet

	Rating	Weight Factor	Item Score
a.	____	× 2 =	____
b.	____	× 2 =	____
c.	____	× 2 =	____
d.	____	× 3 =	____
e.	____	× 3 =	____
		Total =	____
		Total ÷ 12 =	☐ AGS

Scale: 0-not yet attempted　1-beginning planning　2-advanced planning　3-beginning implementation　4-partial implementation　5-advanced implementation

33. Goal Statement (Speech-Impaired Students)

The media specialist develops media center programs responsive to the special needs of speech-impaired students.

The media specialist:

a. Uses spoken language in all activities. 0 1 2 3 4 5

b. Encourages speech-impaired students to speak, if the situation will not cause embarrassment to the student. 0 1 2 3 4 5

c. Listens attentively and patiently to students with speech and language impairments, letting them finish their own sentences. 0 1 2 3 4 5

d. Reads and studies information about speech impairments and their effects on learning. 0 1 2 3 4 5

e. Designs some activities where success is not dependent on speech functioning. 0 1 2 3 4 5

f. Provides activities where the student can experience success in learning to use spoken language. 0 1 2 3 4 5

g. Designs instructional activities which accommodate the individual student's specific language problem. 0 1 2 3 4 5

h. Consults with special education and classroom teachers, speech therapists, parents, students, or others concerning—individual learning styles, strengths/weaknesses, habits/interests, special equipment/material needs, social behavior patterns, degree of impairment/limitations, problems of socialization, and suggested approaches for reaching these students. 0 1 2 3 4 5

Scale: 0-not yet attempted 1-beginning planning 2-advanced planning 3-beginning implementation 4-partial implementation 5-advanced implementation

33. Score Sheet

	Rating	Weight Factor	Item Score
a.	____	× 1 =	____
b.	____	× 1 =	____
c.	____	× 1 =	____
d.	____	× 2 =	____
e.	____	× 2 =	____
f.	____	× 2 =	____
g.	____	× 3 =	____
h.	____	× 3 =	____

Total = ____

Total ÷ 15 = ☐ AGS

34. Score Sheet

	Weight	Item
Rating	Factor	Score

a. _____ × 2 = _____

b. _____ × 2 = _____

c. _____ × 2 = _____

d. _____ × 3 = _____

e. _____ × 3 = _____

Total = _____

Total ÷ 12 = _____   AGS

34. Goal Statement (Orthopedically and Other Health-Impaired Students)

The media specialist develops media center programs responsive to the special needs of orthopedically and other health-impaired students.

The media specialist:

a. Reads and studies information about orthopedic impairments   0 1 2 3 4 5
and other health impairments.

b. Assesses the media center to determine if it is in compliance   0 1 2 3 4 5
with federal regulations for accessibility.

c. Designs some activities where success does not depend on an   0 1 2 3 4 5
area of performance in which the student is disabled.

d. Designs instructional activities which accommodate the indi-   0 1 2 3 4 5
vidual student's specific orthopedic or health impairment.

e. Consults with special education and classroom teachers,   0 1 2 3 4 5
parents, students, or others concerning—individual learning
styles, strengths/weaknesses, habits/interests, special equip-
ment/material needs, social behavior patterns, degree of im-
pairment/limitations, problems of socialization, and suggested
approaches for reaching these students.

Scale: 0-not yet attempted 1-beginning planning 2-advanced planning 3-beginning implementation 4-partial implementation 5-advanced implementation

35. Goal Statement (Mentally Retarded Students)

The media specialist develops media center programs responsive to the special needs of mentally retarded students.

The media specialist:

a. Allows adequate time for students who have a slower rate of learning to complete tasks.   0 1 2 3 4 5

b. Times activities according to the student's interest.   0 1 2 3 4 5

c. Reinforces students for appropriate participation in activities and appropriate social behavior.   0 1 2 3 4 5

d. Reads and studies information about mental retardation.   0 1 2 3 4 5

e. Makes provisions so that responses can take on a variety of forms according to individual skills (e.g., pointing, verbally identifying, or reading).   0 1 2 3 4 5

f. Provides a variety of materials and activities geared at self-care, self-protection, social adjustment, and workskill development.   0 1 2 3 4 5

g. Designs instructional activities which accommodate the individual retarded student's specific learning needs.   0 1 2 3 4 5

h. Consults with special education and classroom teachers, parents, students, others concerning—individual learning styles, strengths/weaknesses, habits/interests, special equipment/material needs, social behavior patterns, degree of impairment/limitations, problems with socialization, and suggested approaches for reaching these students.   0 1 2 3 4 5

35. Score Sheet

	Rating	Weight Factor		Item Score
a.	___	$\times 1 =$		___
b.	___	$\times 1 =$		___
c.	___	$\times 1 =$		___
d.	___	$\times 2 =$		___
e.	___	$\times 2 =$		___
f.	___	$\times 3 =$		___
g.	___	$\times 3 =$		___
h.	___	$\times 3 =$		___

Total = ___

Total $\div$ 16 = [___] AGS

Scale: 0-not yet attempted 1-beginning planning 2-advanced planning 3-beginning implementation 4-partial implementation 5-advanced implementation

36. Goal Statement (Visually Impaired Students)

The media specialist develops media center programs responsive to the special needs of visually impaired students.

The media specialist:

a. Reads and studies information about visual handicaps and their effects on learning.   0 1 2 3 4 5

b. Evaluates the size and quality of visuals being used (e.g., print, pictures, or film) and whether the information is conveyed adequately by visuals alone.   0 1 2 3 4 5

c. Designs some activities where success is not dependent on visual ability.   0 1 2 3 4 5

d. Designs instructional activities which accommodate the individual student's specific visual problem.   0 1 2 3 4 5

e. Consults with special education and classroom teachers, parents, students, or others concerning—individual learning styles, strengths/weaknesses, habits/interests, special equipment/material needs, social behavior patterns, degree of impairment/limitations, problems with socialization, and suggested approaches for reaching these students.   0 1 2 3 4 5

36. Score Sheet

	Rating	Weight Factor	Item Score
a.	___	× 2 =	___
b.	___	× 2 =	___
c.	___	× 2 =	___
d.	___	× 3 =	___
e.	___	× 3 =	___
		Total =	___
		Total ÷ 12 =	☐ AGS

Scale: 0-not yet attempted 1-beginning planning 2-advanced planning 3-beginning implementation 4-partial implementation 5-advanced implementation

37. Goal Statement (Deaf and Hard-of-Hearing Students)

The media specialist develops media center programs responsive to the special needs of deaf and hard-of-hearing students.

The media specialist:

a. Reads and studies information about deaf and hard-of-hearing people. 0 1 2 3 4 5

b. Designs some activities where success is not dependent on hearing acuity. 0 1 2 3 4 5

c. Designs instructional activities which accommodate the individual student's hearing impairment. 0 1 2 3 4 5

d. Consults with special education and classroom teachers, parents, students, or others concerning—individual learning styles, strengths/weaknesses, habits/interests, special equipment/material needs, social behavior patterns, degree of impairment/limitations, problems with socialization, preferred mode of communication, (e.g., oral, signing, or total communication), and suggested approaches for reaching these students. 0 1 2 3 4 5

37. Score Sheet

	Rating	Weight Factor	Item Score
a.	____	× 2 =	____
b.	____	× 2 =	____
c.	____	× 3 =	____
d.	____	× 3 =	____
		Total =	____
		Total ÷ 10 =	☐ AGS

Scale: 0-not yet attempted 1-beginning planning 2-advanced planning 3-beginning implementation 4-partial implementation 5-advanced implementation

38. Goal Statement (Seriously Emotionally Disturbed Students)

The media specialist develops media center programs responsive to the special needs of seriously emotionally disturbed students.

The media specialist:

a. Uses a consistent approach in relating to the individual student.   0 1 2 3 4 5

b. Reads and studies information about emotionally disturbed students and the effect of this disability on learning.   0 1 2 3 4 5

c. Uses a variety of formats to instruct, practice, review, and test.   0 1 2 3 4 5

d. Provides space that is free of distractions and disturbances for concentrated study and activities.   0 1 2 3 4 5

e. Designs instructional activities which accommodate the individual student's specific emotional problem.   0 1 2 3 4 5

f. Consults with special education and classroom teacher, parents, students, or others concerning—individual learning styles, strengths/weaknesses, habits/interests, special equipment/material needs, social behavior patterns, degree of impairment/limitations, problems with socialization, and suggested approaches for reaching these students.   0 1 2 3 4 5

38. Score Sheet

	Rating	Weight Factor		Item Score
a.	_____	× 1	=	_____
b.	_____	× 2	=	_____
c.	_____	× 2	=	_____
d.	_____	× 2	=	_____
e.	_____	× 3	=	_____
f.	_____	× 3	=	_____
			Total =	_____
		Total ÷ 13 =		[ ] AGS

Scale: 0-not yet attempted   1-beginning planning   2-advanced planning   3-beginning implementation   4-partial implementation   5-advanced implementation

PROFILING THE MEDIA CENTER
Graph Profile

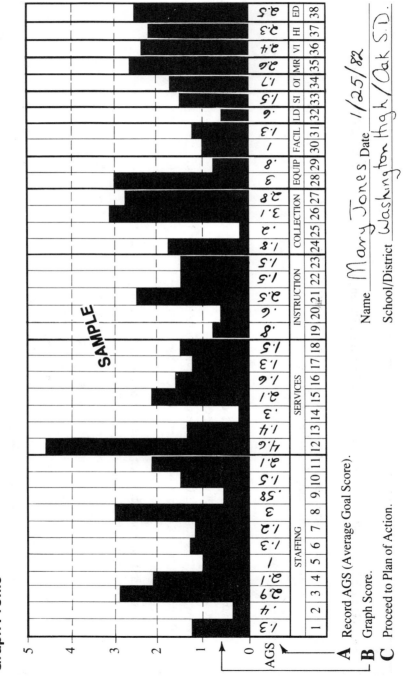

A   Record AGS (Average Goal Score).
B   Graph Score.
C   Proceed to Plan of Action.

Name Mary Jones Date 1/25/82
School/District Washington High/Oak S.D.

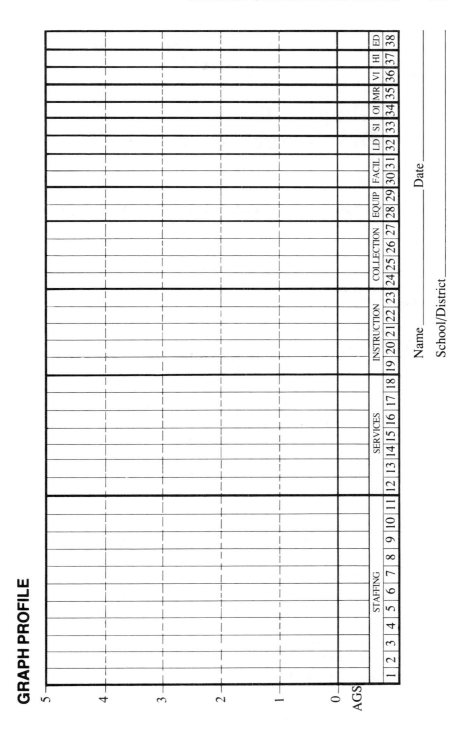

GRAPH PROFILE

AGS

Name _____ Date _____

School/District _____

Chapter 18
Developing a Plan of Action

INSTRUCTIONS FOR DEVELOPING A PLAN OF ACTION

1. After you have graphed your average goal scores (AGS), use your "Graph Profile" and the completed "Assessment Guide" to help you set priorities for those areas on which you want to work. Select those goal statements which reflect the needs of your media center, using such criteria as:

    - What goal statements are a high priority in terms of needing immediate attention? A low AGS does not necessarily indicate a high priority. There may be a good reason for a low score (such as the goal is related to a secondary or elementary school emphasis; or the goal relates to students not taught in your school; or the goal is already handled on a district level; or a need is being met by an alternative program or staff). You may choose items with higher scores if there is a priority to bring a goal up from beginning implementation to full implementation.

    - What effort is required to achieve the goal (time, money, staff, staff coordination, etc.)? This will certainly determine the number of goals you will tackle.

    - What can realistically be planned and implemented during the school year? Select 3–5 goals, depending on the complexity of your activities.

    - What are the projected *needs* of *your* school population? (Perhaps you can obtain information from schools that may feed into your school in order to determine future plans.)

2. For *each* goal statement you have selected, fill out a "Plan of Action" form. (One sheet for each goal statement; number sheets in priority order.) The following instructions correspond with the "Sample Plan of Action" form.

A Fill in the information at the top of each "Plan of Action" form. Fill in media center program areas, which include staffing, services, instruction, collection, equipment, facilities, or specific handicapping conditions.

B Write the selected goal statement in the first column.

C Using the rating scale, interpret your AGS for each goal statement and record its current level of implementation: e.g., not yet attempted; beginning planning, advanced planning, etc.

D Project and record the level of implementation you would like to achieve by the end of the school year.

E The indicators beneath each goal statement in the "Assessment Guide" will become your objectives. Select those indicators (objectives) on which you want to focus. Write them in the objectives column in priority order.

F In the activity column list ideas for implementing the objectives. (Refer to the manual, consult with resource people, media center staff, school administration, parents, students—any resources that will assist you in developing activities.)

G For each activity, write a projected starting date and completion date in the time-line column. Ongoing activities may be so indicated.

SAMPLE PLAN OF ACTION FOR ONE GOAL

PROGRAM AREA: **A** Staffing	SCHOOL Washington High ADDRESS 703 Oak Street Central City, OR 97001	MEDIA SPECIALIST Mary Jones GRADE LEVELS 9-12	DATE 1/30/82

B	**C** current level of implementation	**D** projected level of implementation	**E**	**F**	**G**
GOAL STATEMENT			OBJECTIVES: (INDICATORS)	ACTIVITIES:	TIME-LINE start comp
The Media Specialist builds and maintains a professional Library collection for teachers and staff which includes materials related to mainstreaming.	Not yet attempted	beginning implementation of implementation	places name on mailing lists of various organizations serving the handicapped.	- orders copy of *Directory of National Information Sources* - reviews Directory and selects 10 organizations which offer pertinent and free information on the handicapped. - Send cards to 10 organizations to be placed on mailing List.	5/1 by 9/1 9/7-9 9/10 9/10 9/12
			requests suggestions from teachers etc. for ideas for Collection.	- prepares questionnaire asking for ideas for professional Collection. - distributes at faculty meeting. - collects questionnaires and reviews requests.	9/15 9/16 (make copies) 9/18 9/22 9/24
			circulates to teachers items of interest on the handicapped.	- Designs and orders routing Stamp for Mainstreaming materials. - Uses Stamp when Reviewing mail each day.	9/29 10/6 10/7 —

PLAN OF ACTION FORM

PROGRAM AREA: _____   SCHOOL _____   MEDIA SPECIALIST: _____   DATE _____

ADDRESS _____   GRADE LEVELS _____

GOAL STATEMENT:	OBJECTIVES: (INDICATORS)	ACTIVITIES:	TIME-LINE start | complete

current level of implementation

projected level of implementation

Bibliography

AID: Accepting Individual Differences. Developmental Learning Materials, 7440 Natchez Ave., Niles, IL 60648. (Kit.)

Aiello, Barbara. *The Invisible Children*. Learning Corporation, 1350 Avenue of the Americas, New York, NY 10019. (Film or video cassette.)

Aiello, Barbara, ed. *Places and Spaces: Facilities Planning for Handicapped Children and Adults*. Reston, VA: Council for Exceptional Children, 1976.

American Association of School Librarians. *Media Programs: District and School*. Chicago, IL: American Library Association, 1975.

American Library Association. *Programming for Children with Special Needs*. Chicago, IL: American Library Association, 1980.

American Library Association. *Selecting Materials for Children with Special Needs*. Chicago, IL: American Library Association, 1980.

Amicus. South Bend, IN: National Center for Law and the Handicapped Inc. Bimonthly. 211 W. Washington St., Suite 1900, South Bend, IN 46617.

Anderson, Robert M.; Martinez, David H.; and Lindale, Rick H. "Perspectives for Change." In *Implementing Learning in the Least Restrictive Environment*, ed. John W. Schifani, Robert M. Anderson, and Sara S. Odle. Baltimore, MD: University Park Press, 1980.

Baker, Clifford D., and Fowler, Barbara J. *Preparing General Educators to Work with Handicapped Students*. Greeley, CO: University of Northern Colorado, 1979.

Baker, D. Philip. "Mediacentric." *Wilson Library Bulletin* 53 (2) (October, 1978).

Baker, D. Philip, and Bender, Dave. *Library Media Programs and the Special Learner*. New York: The Shoestring Press, 1981.

Ballard, Joseph. *Public Law 94-142 and Section 504—Understanding What They Are and Are Not*. Reston, VA: Council for Exceptional Children, 1977.

Ballard, Joseph; Nazzaro, Jean N.; and Weintraub, Frederick J. *PL 94-142, The Education for All Handicapped Children Act of 1975.* Reston, VA: Council for Exceptional Children, 1976.

Bardenstein, Linda. *Selection and Adaptation of Media for the Deaf.* Rochester, NY: National Technical Institute for the Deaf, no date.

Baskin, Barbara, and Harris, Karen. *The Exceptional Child in the School Library: Response and Strategy.* Washington, DC: U.S. Educational Resources Information Center, October, 1974. ERIC document ED 097 896.

————. *Notes from a Different Drummer: A Guide to Juvenile Fiction Portraying the Handicapped.* New York: R. R. Bowker Co., 1977.

————, eds. *The Special Child in the Library.* Chicago: American Library Association, 1976.

Berger, Gilda. *Learning Disabilities and Handicaps.* New York: Watts, 1978.

Better Understanding of Disabled Youth (BUDY) (1980). Ideal School Supply, 11000 S. Lavergne Ave., Oak Lawn, IL 60453. (Five multimedia kits.)

Bibliography of Secondary Materials for Teaching Handicapped Students. Washington, DC: President's Committee on Employment of the Handicapped, 1977.

Birch, Jack W. *Hearing Impaired Pupils in the Mainstream.* Reston, VA: Council for Exceptional Children, 1976.

Birch, Jack W. *Mainstreaming: Educable Mentally Retarded Children in Regular Classes.* Reston, VA: Council for Exceptional Children, 1974.

Bleil, Gordon. "Evaluating Educational Materials." *Journal of Learning Disabilities* 8 (1) (January 1975): 12–19.

Briggs, Paul W. "School Media Center Architectural Requirements." *School Media Quarterly* 2 (3) (Spring 1974).

Cary, Jane Randolph. *How to Create Interiors for the Disabled.* New York: Pantheon Books, 1978.

Chisholm, Margaret E., and Ely, Donald P. *Media Personnel in Education.* Englewood Cliffs, NJ: Prentice-Hall, Inc., 1976.

Coons, Maggie, and Milner, Margaret, eds. *Creating an Accessible Campus.* Washington, DC: Association of Physical Plant Administrations of Universities and Colleges, 1978.

Corn, Anne Lesley, and Martinez, Iris. *When You Have a Visually Impaired Child in Your Classroom: Suggestions for Teachers.* NY: American Foundation for the Blind, 1977.

Council for Exceptional Children. *Guidelines for Representation of Exceptional Persons in Educational Media*. Reston, VA: Council for Exceptional Children Publications, 1979.

Coyne, Phyllis. *Resource Booklet on Recreation and Leisure for the Developmentally Disabled*. (Developed for Recreation and Leisure Skills Training Workshop at Portland State University, April 1978).

Davis, Julia, ed. *Our Forgotten Children: Hard-of-Hearing Pupils in the Regular Classroom*. Minneapolis, MN: National Support Systems Project, 1977.

Deno, E. N. *Educating Children with Emotional, Learning and Behavior Problems*. Minneapolis, MN: National Support Systems Project, 1979.

Dresang, Eliza T. "There Are No Other Children." *School Library Journal* 24 (1) (September 1977).

Dreyer, Sharon Spredermann. *The Bookfinder*. Circle Pines, MN: American Guidance Service, 1977.

Fairchild, Thomas N., and Parks, A. Lee. *Mainstreaming the Mentally Retarded Child*. Mainstreaming Series. Boston: Teaching Resources (formerly published at Austin, TX: Learning Concepts, 1977).

Family Relations. Vision, Hearing, and Speech Series (1972). Creative Arts, 2323 4th St., N.E., Washington, DC 20002. (Six 9″ × 11″ prepared transparencies.)

Feeling Free (1979). Scholastic Books, 906 Sylvan Ave., Englewood Cliffs, NJ 07632. (Multimedia kit.)

Freeman, Gerald G. *Speech and Language Services and the Classroom Teacher*. Minneapolis, MN: National Support Systems Project, 1977.

Fusco, Carol B. *Individually Prescribed Program of Instruction for Pupils Who Are Orthopedically Handicapped*. Columbia, SC: South Carolina State Department of Education, 1977. ERIC document ED 140 558.

Gearheart, William R., and Weishahn, Mel. *The Handicapped Child in the Regular Classroom*. St. Louis, MO: Mosby, 1976.

Gilhool, Thomas K. "Changing Public Policies: Roots and Forces." *Minnesota Education* 2 (2) (Winter, 1976): 9–10, 12.

Goldstein, Herbert. "The Role of Media Services in the Education of the Special Student." *Issues in Media Management* (1977): 43.

Guidelines for the Representation of Exceptional Persons in Educational Media. Reston, VA: Council for Exceptional Children. 1979.

Hagerty, Robert, and Howard, Thomas. *How to Make Federal Mandatory Special Education Work for You: A Handbook for Educators and Consumers*. Springfield, IL: Charles C Thomas Publishers, 1978.

Hale, Glorya, ed. *Source Book for the Disabled*. New York: Paddington Press, Ltd., 1979.

Handicapped Requirements Handbook. Washington, DC: Federal Programs Advisory Service. Monthly. 2120 L St., N.W., Suite 210, Washington, DC 20037.

"Handicappism in Children's Books." *Interracial Books for Children Bulletin*. (Double Issue). 8 (6, 7) (1977).

Haring, Norris G., ed. *Behavior of Exceptional Children*. 2d ed. Columbus, OH: Charles E. Merrill, 1978.

Haring, Norris G., and Schiefelbusch, R. L. *Teaching Special Children*. New York: McGraw-Hill Book Co., 1967.

Harris, Karen, and Baskin, Barbara. *The Exceptional Child in the School Library: Identification and Accommodation*. Washington, DC: U.S. Educational Resources Information Center, 1974. ERIC document ED 097 897.

Haskins, James. *Who Are the Handicapped?* New York: Doubleday, 1978.

Heinich, Robert, ed. *Educating All Handicapped Children*. Englewood Cliffs, NJ: Educational Technology Publications, 1979.

Henne, John F. "Serving Visually Handicapped." *School Library Journal* 25 (4) (December, 1978).

Henson, Ferris O., II, and Fairchild, Thomas N. *Mainstreaming Children with Learning Disabilities*. Mainstreaming Series. Boston: Teaching Resources (formerly published at Austin, TX: Learning Concepts, 1977).

I'm Just Like You (1977). Sunburst Communications, Victoria Production, Inc., Pleasantville, NY 10570. (Filmstrip/cassette kit.)

Johnson, David W., and Johnson, Robert T. *Learning Together and Alone: Cooperation, Competition and Individualization*. Minneapolis, MN: University of Minnesota, 1978.

Journal of Learning Disabilities. Chicago, IL: Professional Press. 10 issues per year. 101 E. Ontario St., Chicago, IL 60611.

Journal of Special Education. New York: Grune and Stratton. Quarterly. Subscription Department, 111 Fifth Ave., New York, NY 10003.

Kent, Deborah. "There and Back Again." *Disabled USA*. 1 (7) (1978).

Kids Come in Special Flavors, Box 562, Dayton, OH 45405. (Kit.)

Kliment, Stephen A. *Into the Mainstream: A Syllabus for a Barrier-Free Environment.* NY: American Institute of Architects, 1975.

Konapatske, Pat. Fern Ridge High School, Elmira, OR. Interview, January 1980.

Lake, Sara. *Mainstreaming: A Special Interest Resource Guide in Education.* Phoenix, AZ: Oryx Press, 1980.

Langone, John. *Goodbye Bedlam.* Waltham, MA: Little, Brown, 1974.

Large Type Books in Print. New York: R. R. Bowker Co., 1980.

The Law and Handicapped Children in School. Bloomington, IN: Audiovisual Center, Indiana University, 1979.

McCarr, Dorothy, and Wisser, Mary W., compilers. *Curriculum Materials Useful for the Hearing Impaired.* Beaverton, OR: Dormac, 1979.

McCartan, Kathleen W. *The Communicatively Disordered Child.* Mainstreaming Series. Boston: Teaching Resources (formerly published at Austin, TX: Learning Concepts, 1977.)

McKay, Richard J.; Schwartz, Linda; and Willis, Kathy. "The Instructional Media Center's Function in Programs for Special Needs Children at the Middle School Level." *International Journal of Instructional Media* 4 (1) (1976–77).

Martin, Glenda J., and Hoben, Millie. *Supporting Visually Impaired Students in the Mainstream.* Reston, VA: Council for Exceptional Children, 1977.

Martinez, Dave H. "Learning Disabilities." Unpublished dissertation, Portland State University, 1978.

Matthew and Julie and Spanish Dancer (1975). National Foundation/March of Dimes, 1275 Mamaroneck Ave., White Plains, NY 10605. (Filmstrips.)

"Media/Information/Services for Exceptional Students." *Illinois Libraries.* 59 (September 1977).

Meet Series (1978). H & H Enterprises, Inc., P.O. Box 1070, Lawrence, KS 66044. (Kit with 4 books and matching records: *Meet Lance* [trainable mentally retarded], *Meet Danny* [multiply disabled], *Meet Scott* [learning disabled], and *Meet Camille and Danille* [hearing impaired]).

Miller, Inabeth. "The Micros are Coming." *Media and Methods* (April 1980) 33 ff.

Mimi: This Is Who I Am (1977). Guidance Associates, 757 3rd Ave., New York, NY 10017. (Filmstrip.)

Monson, Dianne, and Shurtleff, Cynthia. "Altering Attitudes toward the Physically Handicapped through Print and Non-Print Media." *Language Arts* 56 (2) (February 1979).

National Education Association (NEA). *The Educable Mentally Retarded Student in the Secondary School*. Washington, DC: National Education Association, 1975.

National Information Center for Educational Media. *NICEM Index to Non-Print Special Education Materials—Multimedia. Learner Volume*. Los Angeles: National Information Center for Educational Media, 1979.

National Information Center for Educational Media. *NICEM Index to Non-Print Special Education Materials—Multimedia. Professional Volume*. Los Angeles: National Information Center for Educational Media, 1979.

Orlansky, Janice Zatzman. *Mainstreaming the Hearing Impaired Child: An Educational Alternative*. Mainstreaming Series. Boston: Teaching Resources (formerly published at Austin, TX: Learning Concepts, 1977).

Orlansky, Michael D. *Mainstreaming the Visually Impaired Child*. Mainstreaming Series. Boston: Teaching Resources (formerly published at Austin, TX: Learning Concepts, 1977).

Parks, A. Lee. *Behavior Disorders: Helping Children with Behavioral Problems*. Mainstreaming Series. Boston: Teaching Resources (formerly published at Austin, TX: Learning Concepts, 1976).

Paul, James L. *Mainstreaming: A Practical Guide*. Syracuse, NY: Syracuse University Press, 1977.

PEACHES (Pre-School Educational Adaptations for Children Who Are Handicapped). *For Your First Days with a Handicapped Child*. Portland, OR: Special Education Department, Portland State University, 1978.

People . . . Just Like You. President's Committee on Employment of the Handicapped, Committee on Youth Development, Washington, DC 20210.

Perceptions. Millburn, NJ: Perceptions, Inc. 8 issues per year. P.O. Box 142, Millburn, NJ 07041.

Petrie, Joyce. *Media and Mainstreaming: An Annotated Bibliography and Related Resources*. Washington, DC: U.S. Educational Resources Information Center. ERIC document ED 190 130.

Pick a Title. Baltimore, MD: The Maryland State Department of Education, 1978.

Please Know Me As I Am. The Jerry Cleary Co., 25 Ronald Rd., Sudbury, MA 01776. (Kit.)

Project STRETCH (1980). Hubbard, 1946 Raymond Dr., Northbrook, IL 60062. (Video/film programs.)

Pursell, Margaret Sanford. *Look at Physical Handicaps.* Minneapolis, MN: Lerner Publishers, 1976.

Put Yourself in My Place (1978). Guidance Associates, Inc., 757 Third Ave., New York, NY 10017. (Filmstrip/cassette kit.)

Reynolds, Maynard C., ed. *Mainstreaming—Origins and Implications.* Reston, VA: Council for Exceptional Children, 1976.

Reynolds, Maynard C. and Birch, Jack W. *Teaching Exceptional Children in All American Schools.* Reston, VA: Council for Exceptional Children, 1977.

"The Role of Media in Special Education." *Audiovisual Instruction* 14 (November 1969).

Ruark, Ardis, and Melby, Carole. *Kangaroo Kapers or How to Jump into Library Services for the Handicapped.* Pierre, SD: Division of Elementary and Secondary Education, 1978.

Sadker, Myra Pollack, and Sadker, David Miller. *Now Upon a Time.* New York: Harper and Row, 1977.

Scanlon, Cheryl, and Almond, Patricia. *Task Analysis and Data Collection.* Portland, OR: ASIEP Educational Co., 1981.

Schrag, Judy A. *Individualized Educational Programming (IEP): A Child Study Team Process.* Mainstreaming Series. Boston: Teaching Resources (formerly published at Austin, TX: Learning Concepts, 1977).

Smith, Pamela Bodoin and Bentley, Glee Ingram. *Participant Manual, Mainstreaming, (Teacher Training Program): Mainstreaming Mildly Handicapped Students into the Regular Classroom.* Austin, TX: Education Service Center, Region XIII, 1975.

"Special Education: A Continuum of Services." *School Media Quarterly* 6 (Summer, 1978).

Stasios, Rosemarie, ed. *HELP for Emotional and Learning Problems.* Toronto, ON: Ontario Teachers' Federation, 1973.

Stephens, Thomas M; Hartman, A. Carol; and Lucas, Virginia H. *Teaching Children Basic Skills: A Curriculum Handbook.* Columbus, OH Charles E. Merrill Publishing Co, 1979.

Stern, Virginia W., and Redden, Martha Ross. "Role Models for the Handicapped." *National Elementary Principal* 58 (1) (October 1978).

Strom, Maryalls G. *Library Service to the Blind and Physically Handicapped*. New York: Scarecrow, 1977.

Teacher Training in Mainstreaming. New York: EPIE (Educational Products Information Exchange) Institute, 1978. EPIE Report: No. 86 m.

"Technology and the Exceptional." *Audiovisual Instruction* 21 (December 1976).

Teen Scenes (1979). Developmental Learning Materials, 7440 Natchez Ave., Niles, IL 60648. (Twelve full color posters 12" × 18".)

Terwilligar, Jane, ed. *Special People, Special Needs, Special Services*. Athens, GA: University of Georgia, Department of Educational Media and Librarianship, 1978. ERIC document ED 157 500.

Thomas, Carol H., and Thomas, James L. *Meeting the Needs of the Handicapped: A Resource for Teachers and Librarians*. Phoenix, AZ: Oryx Press, 1980.

Thomas, N. Angele, ed. *Developing Skills in Severely and Profoundly Handicapped Children*. Reston, VA: Council for Exceptional Children, 1977.

Turnbull, Ann P.; Strickland, Bonnie; and Brantley, John C. *Developing and Implementing Individualized Education Programs*. Columbus, OH: Charles E. Merrill Publishing Co., 1978.

U.S. Department of Health, Education, and Welfare. Office for Handicapped Individuals. *Directory of National Information Sources on Handicapping Conditions and Related Services*. Washington, DC: U.S. Government Printing Office, 1980.

————. *Federal Assistance for Programs Serving the Handicapped*. Washington, DC: U.S. Government Printing Office, 1978.

U.S. Department of Health, Education, and Welfare. Office of Civil Rights. *A Training and Resource Directory for Teachers Serving Handicapped Students, K–12*. Washington, DC: U.S. Government Printing Office, 1977.

U.S. Department of Health, Education, and Welfare. Office of Education. "Assistance to States for Education of Handicapped Children, Procedures for Evaluating Specific Learning Disabilities." *Federal Register* 42, no. 250, 29 December 1977.

————. "Education of Handicapped Children, Implementation of Part B of the Education of Handicapped Act." *Federal Register* 42, no. 163, 23 August 1977.

Vandergrift, Kay E. "Person and Environment." *School Media Quarterly* 4 (4) (Summer 1976).

Velleman, Ruth A. *Serving Physically Disabled People*. New York: R. R. Bowker Co., 1979.

Vernon, McCay. "Deafness and Mental Health: Some Theoretical Views." *Gaullaudet Today* 9 (1) (Fall, 1978).

Weintraub, Frederick J. *State Law and Education of Handicapped Children: Issues and Recommendations*. Reston, VA: Council for Exceptional Children, 1972.

What if You Couldn't . . . ? A Program About Handicaps (1978). Children's Museum of Boston, with WGBH-TV. Burt Harrison and Co., P.O. Box 732, Weston, MA 02193. (Multimedia kit.)

Wise, Bernice Kemler. *Teaching Materials for the Learning Disabled*. Chicago, IL: American Library Association, 1980.

Wright, Kieth C. *Library and Information Services for Handicapped Individuals*. Littleton, CO: Libraries Unlimited, Inc., 1979.

Appendix: Organizations

Academy of Rehabilitative Audiology, Speech and Hearing Science Section, 325 Derby Hall, Department of Communications, Ohio State University, Columbus, OH 43210.

Accent on Information, Inc., Gillum Rd. and High Dr., P.O. Box 700, Bloomington, IL 61701.

Alexander Graham Bell Association for the Deaf (aural/oral), 3417 Volta Pl., N.W., Washington, DC 20007.

American Association for the Education of the Severely/Profoundly Handicapped, 1600 W. Armory Way, Seattle, WA 98119.

American Cancer Society, 777 3rd Ave., New York, NY 10017.

American Coalition of Citizens with Disabilities, 1200 15th St., N.W., Washington, DC 20005.

American Foundation for the Blind, 15 W. 16th St., New York, NY 10011.

American Library Association, Library Services for the Blind and Physically Handicapped, 50 E. Huron St., Chicago, IL 60611.

American Printing House for the Blind, 1839 Frankfort Ave., Louisville, KY 40206.

American Speech and Hearing Association, 10801 Rockville Pike, Rockville, MD 20852.

Arthritis Foundation, 3400 Peachtree Rd., N.E., Suite 1101, Atlanta, GA 30326.

Association for Children with Learning Disabilities, 5225 Grace St., Pittsburgh, PA 15236.

Association for Education of the Visually Handicapped, 919 Walnut St., Fourth Floor, Phildelphia, PA 19107.

Bureau of Education for the Handicapped, Captioned Films and Telecommunications Branch, U.S. Office of Education, Washington, DC 20202.

Captioned Films for the Deaf Distribution Center, 5034 Wisconsin Ave., N.W., Washington, DC 20016.

Center for Innovation in Teaching the Handicapped, Indiana University, 2085 E. 10th St., Bloomington, IN 47401.

Clearinghouse on the Handicapped, 400 Maryland Avenue, S.W., Rm. 3106, Switzer Building, Washington, DC 20202.

Closed-Captioned Television, 1443 Beachwood Dr., Hollywood, CA 90028.

Closer Look Information Center, 1201 16th St., N.W., Washington, DC 20036.

Council for Exceptional Children, 1920 Association Dr., Reston, VA 22091.

Cystic Fibrosis Foundation, 3379 Peachtree Rd., N.E., Atlanta, GA 30326.

Developmental Disabilities Office, U. S. Department of Health and Human Services, 200 Independence Ave., S.W., Washington, DC 20201.

Epilepsy Foundation of America, 1828 L St., N.W., Washington, DC 20036.

Gallaudet College Press (total communication), Kendall Green, N.E., Washington, DC 20002.

Gesell Institute of Child Development, 310 Prospect St., New Haven, CT 06511.

Leukemia Society of America, 211 E. 43rd St., New York, NY 10017.

Mental Health Materials Center, 419 Park Ave., S., New York, NY 10016.

Muscular Dystrophy Association, Inc., 810 7th Ave., New York, NY 10019.

National Association for Retarded Citizens, 2709 Avenue E, East, Arlington, TX 76011.

National Association of the Deaf, 814 Thayer Ave., Silver Springs, MD 20910.

National Association of the Physically Handicapped, 76 Elm St., London, OH 43140.

National Center Education Media and Materials for the Handicapped (NCEMMH), 356 Arps Hall, 1945 N. High St., Ohio State University, Columbus, OH 43210.

National Congress of Organizations of the Physically Handicapped, Inc., 7611 Oakland Ave., Minneapolis, MN 55423.

National Easter Seals Society for Crippled Children and Adults, 2023 W. Ogden Ave., Chicago, IL 60612.

National Foundation/March of Dimes, 1275 Mamaroneck Ave., White Plains, NY 10605.

National Hemophilia Foundation, 25 W. 39th St., New York, NY 10018.

National Information Center for Educational Media (NICEM), University of Southern California, University Park, Los Angeles, CA 90007.

National Library Service for the Blind and Physically Handicapped, Library of Congress, 1291 Taylor St., N.W., Washington, DC 20542.

National Multiple Sclerosis Society, 205 E. 42nd St., New York, NY 10017.

National Society for Autistic Children, 306 31st St., Huntington, WV 25702.

National Support Systems Project, 350 Elliot Hall, University of Minnesota, Minneapolis, MN 55455.

Orton Society, 8415 Bellona Ln., Towson, MD 21204.

The President's Committee on Employment of the Handicapped, Department of Labor, 1111 20th St., N.W., Washington, DC 20210.

President's Committee on Mental Retardation, Department of Health and Human Services, ROB #3m, Rm. 2614, 7th and D Sts., S.W., Washington, DC 20201.

Recording for the Blind, 215 E. 58th St., New York, NY 10022.

Sex Information and Education Council of the U.S. (SIECUS), 137-155 N. Franklin St., Hempstead, NY 11550.

Teaching Resources Corporation, 100 Boylston St., Boston, MA 02116.

Trace Research and Development Center for the Severely Communicatively Handicapped, 1500 Highland Ave., Rm. 314, Madison, WI 53706.

United Cerebral Palsy Association, Inc., 66 E. 34th St., New York, NY 10016.

Index

Compiled by Fred Ramey